GOD
Thought of Everything
Strange
and Slimy

Written by Bonnie Bruno

Illustrated by Kevin Brown

Standard
PUBLISHING
CINCINNATI, OHIO

Dedication

This book is dedicated to my husband, Nick, who has listened to my ramblings about amazing critters, and has survived the crazy schedule associated with yet another writing project. During the research for this book, the two of us have stood under the green-on-green canopy of a rainforest, forded gator-infested swamps, climbed rugged mountains, and survived poisonous spider bites—all without leaving home. *Thanks, Hon.*

Project editor: Greg Holder
Jacket design: Tobias' Outerwear for Books
Interior design: Tobias' Outerwear for Books

Scripture taken from the HOLY BIBLE, NEW INTERNATIONAL READER'S VERSION™. Copyright © 1995, 1996, 1998 by International Bible Society. Used by permission of Zondervan Publishing House. All rights reserved.
ISBN 0-7847-1448-7

09 08 07 06 05 04 03   9 8 7 6 5 4 3 2 1

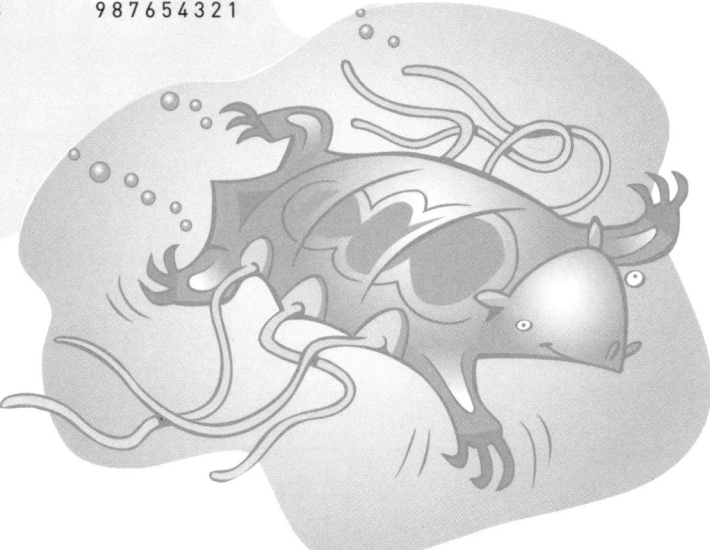

Table of Contents

Wrinkled for a Reason (Giant Chinese Salamander)   8-9

Call Me Talkative, But Please Don't Call Me "Polly!"

    (African Grey Parrot)   10-11

Life in the Slow Lane (Two-Toed Sloth)   12-13

Dressed for Dinner (Himalayan Griffon)   14-15

God Gave Me Goggles (Nile Crocodile)   16-17

A Fair-Weather Forecaster (Giant Grasshopper)   18-19

Watch Your Tongue! (Isopod)   20-21

Behold, the Beached Blob (Portuguese Man-of-War)   22-23

Picnic in the Pond (Leech)   24-25

Ready or Not—Here I Come! (Giant Anteater)   26-27

Following the Crowd (Desert Locust)   28-29

A Skinny, Toothless Wonder (Surinam Toad)   30-31

Beware of Swinging Doors! (Texas Threadsnake)   32-33

Stop 'n Go Fish (Golomyanka)   34-35

Walkin' on Water (African Jacana)   36-37

Sluggish, Slimy, and Special (Banana Slug)   38-39

A Super Stretchy Neck! (Chicken Turtle)   40-41

Hide-and-Seek Hunter (Ambush Bug)   42-43

I've Got My Eye on You! (Giant Vinegaroon)   44-45

When Temperatures Rise (Chuckwalla)   46-47

The Snake That's Never Late (Flying Tree Snake)   48-49

Giant Bell of the Sea (Lion's Mane Jellyfish)   50-51

What a Laugh! (Laughing Kookaburra)   52-53

Diving for Dinner (Fishing Spider)   54-55

A Furry Creature of Habit (Snowshoe Hare)   56-57

Stick 'em Up! (Giant African Stick Insect)   58-59

Today's Special: Savory Insect Stew (Sundew)   60-61

Find Me if You Can! (Ptarmigan)   62-63

The Toughest Little Critter on Earth (Water Bear)   64-65

A Four-Inch Violin (Java Fiddle Beetle)   66-67

Mama Mía, It's a Mamba! (Black Mamba)   68-69

Apartment for Rent (Cecropia Tree)   70-71

Flea on a Pogo Stick (Springtail)   72-73

Life Inside a Chimney (Pompeii Worm)   74-75

My Messy Claim to Fame (White-Throated Woodrat)   76-77

Hairy Ol' What's-His-Name (Camel Spider)   78-79

No Lily Pads for Me! (Wallace's Flying Frog)   80-81

A Sweet Termite Trap (Pitcher Plant)   82-83

When Life Turns Shifty (Jerboa)   84-85

Take Two Mandibles and Call Me in the Morning

     (South American Army Ant)   86-87

Guess Who's Coming for Dinner? (Tarantula Hawk)   88-89

A Hard Nut to Crack (Calvaria Tree)   90-91

My Glow-in-the-Dark Weapon (Giant Red Mysid)   92-93

A Recipe for Trouble: Bounce, Shriek, and Run!

      (Patas Monkey)   94-95

Mighty Mouth of Madagascar

      (Madagascar Hissing Cockroach)   96-97

Orange-Eyed Night Stalker (Eagle Owl)   98-99

Welcome to the Hotel Amazonica (Victoria Amazonica)   100-101

Anteater of the Air (Flying Dragon Lizard)   102-103

Hoses and Gaskets and Wiring, Oh My! (Kea)   104-105

Mini-Hippo, Pig, or Deer? (Babirusa)   106-107

A Naked Tunnel Digger (Naked Mole Rat)   108-109

Hold the Mayo, I'm Not a Tomato! (Tomato Frog)   110-111

A Gentle Aussie Giant (Giant Australian Cuttlefish)   112-113

Too Hot to Handle! (Bombardier Beetle)   114-115

Life Inside the Slime (Slime Worm)   116-117

Stare Down with a Gecko (Ornate Day Gecko)   118-119

Neighborhood Snoop (Carrion Crow)   120-121

My Sticky Zigzag Surprise (Spitting Spider)   122-123

Flightless Parrot of the Night (Kakapo)   124-125

Big Shot of the Forest (Ice Cream Cone Myxo)   126-127

Psssssst! Wanna Know a Secret?

If you have access to the Internet, here's a website especially for you. All 60 links mentioned in this book are available at a special website created by the author. This will save you the headache of having to type every single URL in your browser. Just click on a link and go!

To access the *God Thought of Everything Strange and Slimy* links page, type the following URL in your browser window:

http://www.bonniebruno.com/godthought2.htm

Wrinkled for a Reason

My friends call me Slimy Sal. I'm a 30-inch chocolate-colored critter that looks like something out of a science fiction movie. Most members of my species are just four to six inches long, but at five feet, I'm king of the river. In fact, my appearance is so bizarre, fishermen have tossed their reels into the water when they've accidentally hooked me.

My favorite nesting area is in muddy crevices along the riverbanks here in China. I never just plop down for a nap, though. Instead, God taught me to always lie in my crevice facing outward, in order to both feed and defend myself. Nothing can pass by without my knowing it.

My body gets its needed oxygen from the bubbling waters of fast-moving streams and rivers. The sides of my head and body are covered in deep wrinkles, which capture oxygen-rich water in pools so my body can absorb it.

I am a *nocturnal* hunter, meaning that I hunt only after nightfall.

I lie stone-still in about a foot of water, waiting for a turtle or fish to wander by. Then I explode through the water with my mouth wide open, ready to snatch unsuspecting prey in one big gulp. I also have an appetite for shrimp, snakes, crabs, and frogs. If need be, I am able to open one side of my mouth at a time (can *you* do that?). If my prey is large, I adjust my jaw by bending it forward like a gigantic scoop.

God thought of everything when he created me—**Chinese Giant Salamander.**

More on the Web

Learn more about this giant amphibian at ThinkQuest:
http://library.thinkquest.org/19689/data/amphibians/chinese_salamander_frame.html

Tell a Friend

No matter what our size, we can become a "giant" in God's eyes. How? By reading and obeying his Word, and sharing his love with those around us.

Read About It

"Lord, you are everything I need. I have promised to obey your words."—Psalm 119:57

Pray About It

Lord, I want to obey your Word. Give me the courage to stand up tall for you.

Here in China, I am considered a delicacy at local fish markets.

Call Me Talkative, But Please Don't Call Me "Polly!"

Elegant ladies of the 1800s used to dress up in their finest clothes, then take formal portraits with parrots like me. In those days, ships would bring parrots from our homeland in Africa to Europe. They'd stuff us into small compartments that were much too cramped. Life was unfair.

Today, I have been called a perfect mixture of brains and beauty, but don't ask me to chirp, "Polly want a cracker?" *Harrumph!* Yes, I am a parrot, but my history goes back much farther than Polly. I am like a tape recorder and can repeat multiple lines of songs or prayers. God gave me the rare ability to imitate speech and sounds. If a phone rings, I can copy the ring. The same is true if I hear a chainsaw or microwave running. And watch out—I will repeat messages on an answering machine again and again.

Although my cousins are spread across the world, I live in the lowland forests of central Africa. I move to the open country to feed with my flock. We fly high above treetops screeching. You would never guess we are shy birds.

We lunch on nuts, fruits, berries, and seeds. We climb from one branch to another, and save most of our flying for the return trip to our roosting tree. Members of my species live to 70 years of age or older.

God thought of everything when he created me—**African Grey Parrot.**

More on the Web
Some African grey parrots are born with patches of red:

http://www.wingscc.com/aps/g-red.htm

Tell a Friend
This parrot is entertaining, but doesn't know that sometimes it's better to be quiet. The same is true for us when we pray. Try talking less and instead spending more time in silence. Think about God's love and forgiveness, and give thanks for all he's done for you.

Read About It
"Be still, and know that I am God. I will be honored among the nations. I will be honored in the earth."—Psalm 46:10

Pray About It
Lord, knowing you is an awesome thought! Please remind me to turn off the chatter and listen to you when I pray.

One of my relatives was captured in 1958 near Uganda, and by 1977 he had a vocabulary of nearly 1,000 words!

Life in the Slow Lane

I'm almost 20 years old, and have seen a lot of seasons come and go. My mother gave birth to me here in the tropical forest of Central America while hanging upside down from a tree! At birth, I weighed less than a pound and measured 10 inches. Now I'm about the size of a large house cat.

Each of my hairs is grooved, which allows algae to grow into the grooves and form a nice slimy layer on my fur. Algae turns my coat green and helps me blend in with my green surroundings. My grooved hair, in turn, gives algae a place to get closer to sunlight.

My body systems run extremely slowly, so I don't need a lot of food and water. I live mostly off tasty twigs, leaves, and buds that are within reach. I am a homebody and spend most of my time hanging upside-down from a tree branch. The only way I can get around on solid ground is to reach forward, grab a firm toehold, and drag my body along the ground. I wouldn't stand a chance down there with a

hungry jaguar!

My stomach has many compartments to digest my favorite food—tough twigs. My teeth grow continuously because I wear them down by chewing the twigs. I also enjoy snacking on leaves, buds, fruit, and small prey.

God thought of everything when he created me—**Two-Toed Sloth.**

More on the Web

Visit a sloth picture gallery online:

http://jajhs.kana.k12.wv.us/amazon/sloth.htm

Tell a Friend

Have you ever had a great idea, but given up because it felt like too much work? Don't be like the sloth, who just hangs around all day biding his time. Make your days count by committing each one to God and asking him what he has for you to accomplish.

Read About It

"Commit to the Lord everything you do. Then your plans will succeed."—Proverbs 16:3

Pray About It

Thank you, God, for the gift of life. Help me to pay attention to what you have for me to do.

In the King James Version of the Bible, Proverbs 18:9 compares a sloth to a lazy person who doesn't want to work.

Dressed for Dinner

I am a member of a species called vultures. On a rocky ledge far above the Himalayan tree line, I make my home in a nest woven of sticks. The Himalayas have been called the place where earth meets sky, and what a view I have!

I'm sure no canary! I measure nearly three feet long, with a wingspan of almost 10 feet. I tip the scales at about 15 pounds—as much as a Thanksgiving turkey! Although I'm strong and speedy, I don't hunt alone. Instead, I fly with a group that hovers in the air to stake out our next meal. My victim isn't hard to catch, because my species feasts only on *carcasses*, which are the bodies of dead animals.

That might sound like a disgusting way to find a meal, but we play an important role in cleaning up the countryside. A group of us can pick a carcass apart in a few hours using our sharp, hooked bills. By ridding the land of carcasses, we help prevent the spread of dis-

ease. Although I often feast on animals that have died of diseases, I remain healthy because God gave me a special resistance to illness.

God knows how cold the temperatures get at an elevation of two miles up, so guess what he did? He provided a long layer of soft, warm feathers that surround my neck like a warm ruffle.

God thought of everything when he created me—**Himalayan Griffon.**

More on the Web
Here's a photo of me perched on the edge of a cliff, ready to take off:

http://www.geocities.com/abi_tamim/birds/hymlgrfn.jpg

Tell a Friend
The Himalayan griffon picks apart a carcass for survival. Sometimes in the heat of anger, our words can pick someone apart, too. Spoken out of anger or jealousy, words have the power to kill someone's confidence and make them feel unloved or unlovely. Have you ever been on the receiving end of an angry outburst? How did you handle it?

Without God, many people live in fear and blame God for their problems. The Bible speaks of them as people who wander around "like food for vultures" (Job 15:23).

Read About It
"Those who talk a lot are likely to sin. But those who control their tongues are wise."—Proverbs 10:19

Pray About It
Lord, help me to choose words that help, not hurt.

15

God Gave Me Goggles

I developed in a nest that my mother dug in the backwoods near a river. There she laid a few dozen eggs, then covered the nest with leaves and other debris. The covering kept her babies-to-be warm and safe as they grew. For three months she carefully guarded her eggs—even to the point of skipping meals.

One day, the other hatchlings and I broke out of our shells and announced our arrival with high-pitched chirps. Our mother and father both sprang into action, digging to reach us. They gently rolled any unhatched eggs between their teeth and the roof of their mouths to help free the hatchlings.

In the early weeks of life, my mother carried us around in a pouch under her lower jaw. My parents worked together to protect us for about two years. During that time, they taught us how to live on our own.

I have a lizard-like shape and a rough, scaly hide. But I'm much

bigger than a lizard and will grow up to 20 feet long. Unlike lizards, I do not shed my skin. As I grow larger, my skin grows with me.

My ears and nostrils close when I dive underwater. God also created a second pair of eyelids for me. These see-through eyelids drop down to cover my eyes when I dive or swim. Thanks to God's design, I can see underwater without getting murky water in my eyes. Don't you wish you had built-in swimming goggles like mine?

God thought of everything when he created me—**Nile Crocodile.**

More on the Web

Learn fast facts about the Nile crocodile:

http://www.seaworld.org/AnimalBytes/crocodileab.html

Tell a Friend

God gave the Nile crocodile special eyes to see underwater. When we ask Jesus into our lives, the Bible says we become a new creation. It's like gaining a new set of eyes that can help us view the world differently.

Read About It

"Anyone who believes in Christ is a new creation. The old is gone! The new has come!"
—2 Corinthians 5:17

I have been known to gallop on dry land at speeds up to 29 miles per hour. If I were a car driving in your neighborhood, I might get a speeding ticket!

Pray About It

Dear God, help me to see the wonderful things you have for me in your world.

A Fair-Weather Forecaster

When insect experts discovered me, they called me one of the most striking insect finds of the century. I belong to a family called *giant weta*. It's my family name, just like your last name.

I hail from New Zealand, where I make myself at home in secondhand tunnels. A large beetle that doesn't live here anymore dug the home I currently live in. If I can't locate a ready-made apartment, I'll settle for a warm, dry crevice near the edge of a building. I'll also snuggle inside a hollow tree or the hollow stem of a plant.

God taught me how to protect myself. I'm covered in a scaly suit of armor and I only enter my hollow home headfirst. My spiny hind legs block the entrance to the passage behind me so nothing can follow me inside. Smart trick, don't you think?

My antennae are twice the length of my body. Every evening before I go outside to hunt, I slowly back out of the tunnel. Sensory organs on my rear end can tell whether it's cold, warm, wet, or dry.

I only hunt at night, so if the weather sounds good I'll venture out. My favorite kind of night is warm, damp, and dark.

God thought of everything when he created me—**Giant Grasshopper.**

More on the Web
Giant grasshoppers exist in a lot of different countries. Here are photos of a different species from my family who live in Australia.

http://www.geocities.com/pchew_brisbane/GiantGrassH.htm

Tell a Friend
If weather conditions aren't perfect, the giant grasshopper stays inside. Some friendships change almost as often as the weather. A "fair-weather" friend is loyal only when things suit him or her. What kind of a friend are *you*?

Read About It
"Even a man who has many companions can be destroyed. But there is a friend who sticks closer than a brother."—Proverbs 18:24

Pray About It
Lord, help me to be a faithful friend—one who is kind-hearted, forgiving, and loyal—just like Jesus!

The Bible mentions some of my hungry cousins in Psalm 78:46: "He gave their crops to the grasshoppers. He gave their food to the locusts."

19

Watch Your Tongue!

I'm a member of a group that includes sow bugs and pill bugs. I don't live on land as they do, but in the deep waters of the Gulf of California. You won't find me sunning myself in a shoreline tide pool, either. My life is much busier than that.

I make my home inside the mouth of a fish called the spotted rose snapper. I'm picky about where I live, and you won't find me accepting room and board with any other type of fish. I'm not tagging along for the ride, either. I attach myself to my host's tongue and suck blood for nourishment. I suck so much blood, in fact, the snapper's tongue eventually shrivels up and dies, leaving behind a stub.

But hey, I'm not heartless! I don't desert my host in its hour of need. I stick around—literally. Using hook-like arms on my underside, I clamp onto the stub and take over the duties of a tongue. My host can count on me to help it grab food. When I'm hungry, I snack on bits of floating food.

I'm known as a parasite, because I live off my spotted rose snapper. Once I take over as its tongue, it's a partnership to the end!

God thought of everything when he created me—**Isopod.**

More on the Web

See the handsome fellow in the middle photo? That's my host—a red snapper. I'm the one snuggled inside its mouth.

http://tolweb.org/tree?group=Isopoda&contgroup=Peracarida

Tell a Friend

The spotted rose snapper doesn't know to guard its tongue. If it did, that clingy isopod would not have a chance! The Bible teaches about the importance of guarding our tongues, too. Do you think before you speak, or say things that hurt others?

Read About It

"Anyone who is careful about what he says keeps himself out of trouble."—Proverbs 21:23

I'm the only known parasite that actually replaces an important body part of its host.

Pray About It

Lord, help me to guard my tongue, and to use it to speak words that encourage.

Behold, the Beached Blob

I'm a jelly-like sea animal with a body that resembles a clear plastic bag. Filled with gas, I float on the surface of the water, pushed along by the waves and wind. Members of my family live in the warm waters of the world. People have reported seeing up to 1,000 of us floating together!

I am blue, but some of us are shades of pink, too. We grow anywhere from three to 12 inches.

My underside contains coiled tentacles that can grow up to 165 feet long! I use my tentacles to capture prey: crayfish, plankton, and small fish. I grab them and paralyze them with a sting. My sting is like a shot of poison, and is said to be almost as powerful as the venom of a cobra!

Since I spend my life floating, I have no way of controlling where I end up. God knew I would need direction in my life, so he designed a special body part called a *crest*. My crest looks like a sail. The wind

catches my crest and floats me from place to place. When waves knock me around, I use my muscles to pull myself back up again.

To keep my body from drying out, I dip my crest in the water often. Sometimes accidents happen, and strong winds push some of us ashore.

God thought of everything when he created me—**Portuguese Man-of-War.**

More on the Web

Discover fun facts about this floating creature and click to color a picture of it at Enchanted Learning online.

http://www.enchantedlearning.com/paint/subjects/invertebrates/jellyfish/Manofwar.shtml

Tell a Friend

God controls the direction of the winds that push the Portuguese man-of-war along. His Word gives us direction for our lives, too.

Read About It

"'I know the plans I have for you,' announces the Lord. 'I want you to enjoy success. I do not plan to harm you. I will give you hope for the years to come.'"—Jeremiah 29:11

If you ever spot me washed up on a beach, do not touch me! I may look dead, but I am still able to give a painful, poisonous sting.

Pray About It

Lord, help me to listen to your voice, and to hear the plans you have for my life.

Picnic in the Pond

W ould you be able to go a whole year without eating? I can—if I
have to. As I feed on turtles, frogs, and certain insects, my body
swells nearly five times its normal size. Most days, you'll find me at
the bottom of a pond, feasting on things that have died there. I look
like a flattened worm, and can move through the water like a snake.

God gave me a suction-cup mouth and suction cups on my tail. If
I want to travel on the surface of the water, I attach my mouth to a log
or rock, push forward, and then use my tail suckers in the same way.
I look like a bicycle wheel rolling slowly along. I have strong jaws and
sharp mouthparts to pierce the skin of my prey. My saliva contains a
special painkiller, and a chemical that prevents my victim's blood
from clotting and forming a scab. I feast on a meal of blood and other
body fluids.

In certain cases, doctors have used members of my family to
help certain types of patients. When a badly burned person needs a

skin graft, for example, a blood-sucking cousin of mine is able to help rid the damaged area of excess blood. This causes blood to flow normally until new blood vessels, called *capillaries*, can take over. Patients heal more quickly, thanks to my busy cousin.

God thought of everything when he created me—**Leech.**

More on the Web

Visit a leech farm, where people raise these blood-sucking critters!

http://yucky.kids.discovery.com/noflash/worm/pg000219.html

Tell a Friend

Problems are like leeches. They make us worry day and night. Worry has the power to suck our energy and enthusiasm, but there's good news: God is ever near, ready to rescue us from worry.

Read About It

"I tell you, do not worry...But put God's Kingdom first. Do what he wants you to do." —Matthew 6:25,33

Pray About It

Lord, when worry attaches itself to me, remind me that you are as close as a prayer.

Some members of my family live in the nasal passages of horses, but I prefer the bottom of a murky pond.

Ready or Not— Here I Come!

Think of your favorite snack, and multiply it by 30,000. That's how many ants and termites I can eat in a single day. Before I learned to hunt, I depended on my mother for everything. Even though I could move around in a slow gallop at four weeks after birth, I spent almost a year clinging to my mother's back. She protected me from big wild cats like jaguars and pumas.

God designed my head in a tube shape with a long, slender snout. He equipped me with sharp claws to rip open ant nests. Just as you use your tongue to lick ice cream cones, I use mine for locating insects inside their nests. God knew how deep some of these termite and ant mounds can be, so he gave me a two-foot-long tongue! Once I tear into a tall termite or ant mound, my "super tongue" flits in and out of the nest so fast, insects can't escape.

I live alone in the grasslands of South America. All day long I search for food, and my sharp sense of smell and hearing help me to locate insects quickly.

Of course, I can't hunt all the time. At night, I dig a little hollow in the soft soil and curl up to sleep. Sometimes I use the deserted burrow of another animal, too. My long, bushy tail helps keep me warm like a built-in blanket.

God thought of everything when he created me—**Giant Anteater.**

More on the Web

Learn about all kinds of anteaters in this Amazon Jungle Adventure!

http://jajhs.kana.k12.wv.us/amazon/anteat1.htm

Tell a Friend

God equipped the anteater with an extra-long tongue for hunting. What body parts do you most appreciate? Thank God for equipping you with exactly what you need.

Read About It

"How you made me is amazing and wonderful. I praise you for that. What you have done is wonderful. I know that very well."

—Psalm 139:14

I am the largest and best-known species of ant-eating animals. Covered with gray, bristly hair, I can grow over six feet long. My tail alone measures three feet!

Pray About It

Lord, thank you for equipping me with all that I need to live. Help me to use my body in a way that pleases you.

Following the Crowd

Long before I was able to hop or fly, I grew inside an egg pod. My egg was the size of a grain of rice. A frothy mixture covered me until I hatched into a tiny nymph. Several changes and about two months later, I became an adult.

I live in a dry area of northern Africa. Some members of my family travel alone at night, but I am from a species that migrates from place to place. A *plague* happens when billions of us band together to cover a wide area of land. A group of us is called a swarm, and can spread quickly into as many as 60 countries, eating every plant in our path.

I was designed for movement. God gave me the ability to jump 10 times my body length in one leap! A waxy layer covers my entire body, preventing moisture from evaporating in the hot, dry climate where I live. He taught me how to follow the wind currents. My swarm knows when to leave, and how to stay on course. We progress at about 12

miles per hour, and can travel as far as 80 miles per day.

One report claims that in 1950, swarms of us were tracked from the Arabian Peninsula to the west coast of Africa in less than two months. That's over 3,000 miles!

God thought of everything when he created me—**Desert Locust.**

More on the Web

Locust swarms are monitored constantly. Read the latest at the Desert Locust Information Service website.

http://www.fao.org/NEWS/GLOBAL/LOCUSTS/Locuhome.htm

Tell a Friend

The desert locust spends a lifetime following the crowd. If the swarm turns left, it turns left. When the group speeds up, it speeds up. Do you follow a crowd, like the locust, and let friends make all your decisions? Be very careful who you follow and where they lead you.

Read About It

"Teach me to do what you want, because you are my God. May your good Spirit lead me on a level path."—Psalm 143:10

The Bible is filled with verses about me. Read Exodus 10 to see what happened when Pharaoh refused to free the Israelites from slavery in Egypt.

Pray About It

Dear Lord, help me to remember that following you is always the best course.

A Skinny, Toothless Wonder

I live in muddy canals, swamps, and slow-flowing rivers like the Amazon. If you could peer down into my murky brown home, you'd find me sitting motionless in the mud, waiting to snatch an earthworm, minnow, or other small water creatures. Covered with tiny sensory hairs, my star-shaped fingers help me locate food quickly.

If a small fish tries to sneak by, my mouth turns into a vacuum cleaner. I don't have a tongue or teeth, but God taught me how to expand my body, lunge forward, and suck in passing fish. If the fish is too large, I use my front legs to turn it around until I can swallow it whole. I am able to stay underwater for up to an hour at a time.

I announce my territory by making clicking noises. If an enemy or another toad ventures too close, my clicking turns frantic and I will fight to protect my territory. My back legs are powerful, allowing me

to push through the water at high speeds.

When I'm not hunting, I like to float on the warm surface of the water. Although I'm surrounded by liquid, I don't ever drink water. Instead, my skin acts as a sponge, absorbing water into my body.

God thought of everything when he created me—**Surinam Toad.**

More on the Web

View a spectacular photo album of the Surinam toad at the Honolulu Zoo website!

http://www.honoluluzoo.org/surinam_toad_gallery.htm

Tell a Friend

The Surinam toad is surrounded by water, yet never drinks any of it. In the same way, our lives are surrounded by choices—both good and bad. The Bible helps us make wise choices. It is a special guidebook—a gift from God. Have you thanked him for it lately?

Read About It

"Anyone who gets wisdom loves himself. Anyone who values understanding succeeds."—Proverbs 19:8

I'm a toad, but don't look much like one. Rectangular with a flat-topped head, I am often mistaken for a leaf floating in the water.

Pray About It

Sometimes I feel confused, Lord, and don't know which way to turn. Thank you for providing clear instructions through your Word.

Beware of Swinging Doors!

Most snakes devour their victims by opening their mouths as wide as possible, and working each side slowly around and over their prey.

I have my own way of swallowing my prey. Because of my size I avoid antelopes and rats, in favor of ants. At seven inches long, and as thick as a strand of spaghetti, I am the shortest snake in the world.

God knew that my craving for ants would take me inside narrow passageways. A normal snake would not be able to spread its mouth open wide down there, but my Creator designed a special lower jaw that allows me to maneuver in tight spots and eat quickly.

It is equipped with six sets of teeth. Built with three joints—at the chin, and at either side—the jaw divides in the middle, yet both sides work together. Each half bends in, then out, and has been compared to a set of swinging doors. They swing open then close quickly, raking

ants and larvae into my mouth. Researchers watched me dropping and retrieving my jaw flaps at the rate of four times per second.

The faster I eat, the faster I can exit the nest before the ants turn on me. If a band of angry ants were to corner me, I wouldn't stand a chance because of my size.

God thought of everything when he created me—**Texas Threadsnake.**

More on the Web

View a cutaway drawing of my triple-jointed jaw:

http://www.johnmacneill.com/PS_Snake.html

Tell a Friend

The threadsnake's jaw has been compared to swinging doors. That's a good way to describe the mouth of a person who gossips, too. Out goes the rumor; in comes the feedback. Once spoken, words cannot be taken back. "Think before you speak" is a good motto to live by.

Read About It

"With our tongues we praise our Lord and Father. With our tongues we call down curses on people. We do it even though they have been created to be like God. Praise and cursing come out of the same mouth."—James 3:9, 10.

While most snakes take hours to consume their victim, I can eat an entire meal in seconds!

Pray About It

Heavenly Father, help me to be aware of the weight of my words, and that others are affected by what I say.

Stop 'n Go Fish

y mother gave birth to me one autumn in Lake Baikal, Siberia. Females of my species don't lay eggs; their offspring are live, fully developed little fish, called *fries*. I knew how to swim immediately after birth.

My family doesn't travel in large schools. From early on, I lived a solitary life. I also learned how to adjust to the pressure of life at 700 to 1600 feet deep. Way down deep, everything is viewed in black and white. When I journey down in the water, I stop to let my body adjust to the changing water pressure and temperature. Every night I make a trip up to the water's surface, stopping along the way when needed. I return to the depths in the morning.

My body is extremely sensitive to any temperature change. To me, the perfect water temperature is 41 degrees. If the water warms up to 50 degrees, I could die.

I don't have scales like other fish, and my body is made of

about 30 percent oil, rich in Vitamin A. Although I am not fit for eating, my flesh is in demand for other purposes. Long ago, members of my species were picked up on the beaches after a big storm. The fat was melted and used in treatments for arthritis, heart disease, and for healing wounds—all practices that have made me a sought-after fish even today. Native Siberians still use my fat for their oil lamps and for medicine.

God thought of everything when he created me—**Golomyanka.**

More on the Web

Learn more about Lake Baikal—my home—and the friends who share the waters with me.

http://www.baikal.eastsib.ru/baikalfacts/

Tell a Friend

The golomyanka lives with extreme pressure, but God taught it when to stop and rest. Are you feeling pressured by a problem or a busy schedule? God has a solution in the verse below.

Read About It

"Turn all your worries over to him. He cares about you."—1 Peter 5:7

Pray About It

Dear God, when life gets hectic, help me to stop everything and turn to you for help.

My species is the most plentiful fish in Lake Baikal. We account for about 150,000 tons of fish.

Walkin' on Water

My mother laid a clutch of four eggs in a damp nest in South Africa. Four days in a row, at around 7 a.m., she would lay an egg. One of those glossy brown eggs belonged to me!

My father took care of me long before I was born. He guarded the nest for about 25 days. On bright, sunny days, he would check to make sure the eggs stayed a perfect temperature. If he found the eggs too warm, he would move them into the shade; too cool, and he'd sit on them until their temperature increased.

Shortly after I hatched, my father tucked the other three hatchlings and me under his wings. He kept us warm and dry, carrying us around until we were a couple of weeks old.

My claim to fame is my toes. I have the longest toes of any bird, and they help me get a firm grip on floating water plants.

When I land on water, I keep my wings raised slightly and I swoop in like a water plane. Scientists have studied my flying and

landing style, and noticed that I never raise my wings when landing on dry land. God taught me to raise my wings for balance only when I land on water. Otherwise, I would sink.

God thought of everything when he created me—**African Jacana.**

More on the Web

Learn more about the jacana.

http://www.jacana.demon.co.uk/jacana/jac9.htm

Tell a Friend

The jacana's father watched over it long before it hatched, but we have a heavenly Father who knew us personally long before we drew our first breath—and loved us.

Read About It

"None of my bones were hidden from you when you made me inside my mother's body. That place was as dark as the deepest parts of the earth. When you were putting me together there, your eyes saw my body even before it was formed." —Psalm 139:15, 16

God created the eggshell in which I developed with special pores to rid itself of excess moisture. He knew that I'd need a way to stay warm and dry in the wet surroundings of the African floodplain.

Pray About It

Heavenly Father, thank you for watching over me before I was born, and all the days of my life!

Sluggish, Slimy, and Special

Y ou will not find me sunning myself on a hot rock, or slithering around the base of a cactus. I live only on the damp, foggy forest floor of the west coast of the United States. Small holes on the side of my head help me breathe in that cool, damp air. *Ahhhh!*

I might be sluggish, but I'm certainly not lazy! I spend my whole life cleaning the forest floor. My droppings contain a high percentage of nitrogen—something the gigantic redwood trees need to survive. I never, ever eat any part of a redwood tree. However, I *will* chomp away on any plant that competes with the towering redwood. I need the redwood forest, and it needs me!

God blessed me with two sets of antennae on my head. The longer set allows me to watch where I'm going. The shorter set of antennae is for smell. If my antennae are broken off, it's not a big

deal. They will grow back in two days!

In such quiet, peaceful surroundings, you'd think I'd be left alone. But no—predators like snakes, ducks, salamanders, and foxes keep me on my toes. Well, they would if I actually *had* toes! Instead of toes, I have a special muscle on the bottom of my body, called a *foot*. It helps me belly crawl through the forest. When an enemy threatens me, I cover myself in a thick layer of slime. That shuts down their appetite in a hurry!

God thought of everything when he created me—**Banana Slug.**

More on the Web

Other types of slugs inhabit the world's seas:

http://webrum.uni-mannheim.de/klin/seifarth/www/slugsite.html

Tell a Friend

The banana slug uses slime as a protective covering. We do not have to fear when trouble comes our way. God's promises cover us like a blanket.

Read About It

"You are my place of safety. You are like a shield that keeps me safe. I have put my hope in your word."—Psalm 119:114

As I slither along, I mark the path with my scent, so I can find my way home after dark. I also use a slime trail to find fellow slugs.

Pray About It

God, it is amazing to see how you protect even a slimy slug. Thank you for protecting me with your powerful Word—the Bible.

A Super Stretchy Neck

Why does a turtle cross the road? To get to the other side—of course! And, if it happens to be spring or summer, a turtle might be looking for a spot in which to lay its eggs. I don't nest during those seasons, though. I'm different from most turtles. I lay my eggs in cooler months, and spend the winter buried underground.

You will recognize me by a pattern of yellow lines against my green shell. My head, extra-long neck, hind legs, and tail are covered with yellow stripes, too. I live in swampy areas, ponds, ditches, or small lakes. Sometimes I travel overland to hardwood forests. My favorite snack here in the swamps and ponds of Florida is crayfish.

When I was born, I only measured one inch across—about the size of a small walnut. I grew to 10 inches, but some of my cousins only reach six to seven inches. God gave me the longest neck of any turtle! My neck helps me capture small animals. Stretched to its full length, it looks like the neck of a chicken.

God thought of everything when he created me—**Chicken Turtle.**

More on the Web
Find the chicken turtle among this handsome group!

http://www.auburn.edu/academic/science_math/res_area/herpetology/turtles/testudinidae.htm

Tell a Friend
If the chicken turtle never stuck its neck out, it would have to settle for eating crayfish the rest of its days. It would not be able to reach anything bigger than that. If fear prevents us from trying something new, it is often said that we are "afraid to stick our neck out." What about you? Is fear keeping you from doing something big?

Read About It
"Be strong and brave. Do not be terrified. Do not lose hope. I am the Lord your God. I will be with you everywhere you go."—Joshua 1:9

Pray About It
Lord, help me to trust you for each step, and to "stick my neck out" courageously.

If you ever see me crossing a road and want to help, approach me with caution! I'm timid, and if you startle me, I might bite.

Hide-and-Seek Hunter

What's greenish yellow with a wide, dark band across its abdomen? Me, of course! I'm a sneaky bug—a skilled hunter who uses surprise to get what I want. I hide on clusters of flowers that match my colors perfectly. I'm greenish yellow, and I blend right in with a plant called goldenrod. Goldenrod flowers make a perfect hiding place for a hungry critter like me.

God fashioned special front legs for hunting. I wait on a flower for a suitable meal, such as a butterfly, bee, or wasp. The middle section of my front legs, called the *femur*, is thicker than the rest of my leg. Strong muscles work to control a claw-like section below. I can hold onto a fly twice my weight!

God knew that I wouldn't be able to hold onto a wriggly insect forever, so he came up with a quick solution: a thin beak that folds up under my head when not in use. It works like a needle, injecting a poisonous fluid into my victim. The fluid paralyzes it and starts to dis-

God Thought of Everything Strange and Slimy

solve its insides. I then use my beak as a drinking straw to suck up the tasty liquid.

I might sound like an insect to avoid, but gardeners think highly of me. I help keep the population of aphids, scales, and other plant-eating bugs down.

God thought of everything when he created me—**Ambush Bug.**

More on the Web

Here I am, drinking my latest liquid meal:

http://www.chaparraltree.com/mn/amb-beetle-med.shtml

Tell a Friend

Friends do not ambush each other! They do not wait for opportunities to attack unfairly. When problems come up in a friendship, handle it the way Jesus would—fairly and with kindness.

Read About It

"You are God's chosen people. You are holy and dearly loved. So put on tender mercy and kindness as if they were your clothes." —Colossians 3:12

The Bible talks about a different kind of ambush. Read Psalm 64 to learn how God protects those who trust in him.

Pray About It

Dear God, show me how to love others the way you do. Thank you for your mercy and kindness toward me.

I've Got My Eye on You!

I'm slower than a cricket, and I'm not the most skilled hunter in the insect world. My eyesight is poor, and I grope around in the darkness—hardly an insect to raise hairs on the back of your neck.

At three inches long, I might look like a scorpion off some old cowboy movie, but I am a pussycat compared to my poisonous cousin. I'm a member of a species called *whip scorpions*, because of my whip-like tail. I have strong pincers, which I use to shred my victim and transfer its flesh to my mouth. I can deliver a painful pinch, too, if they don't hold still! At the base of my tail lie a couple of glands where a vinegar-scented spray is produced. The acid spray can burn or sting anyone who tries to mess with me.

I am commonly found in desert areas of the southwestern United States. I sometimes venture into grasslands, pine forests, and mountain regions, too. I spend much of my time burrowed under logs and rocks. I keep a close eye on my surroundings. In fact, God gave me

eight eyes—two in the middle, and three on each side of the head! I hide by day and hunt by night. Darkness does not pose a problem, because I have two long feelers that are constantly on guard. I use my feelers to sense vibrations in the area.

God thought of everything when he created me—**Giant Vinegaroon.**

More on the Web

Brace yourself for some close-up photos of yours truly.

http://mamba.bio.uci.edu/~pjbryant/biodiv/spiders/Mastigoproctus.htm

Tell a Friend

Looks can be deceiving, and the vinegaroon is not as harmful as it looks. God instructs us to look inside a person, not at how they dress or where they live. After all, that's how God treats each of us.

Read About It

"I do not look at the things people look at. Man looks at how someone appears on the outside. But I look at what is in the heart."
—1 Samuel 16:7

A railroad camp in early-day Texas was named after me. When the railroads pushed further west, Vinegaroon was soon deserted.

Pray About It

Thank you for seeing me for who I can become in your sight, Lord—not how I look. Remind me of that whenever I meet someone new.

When Temperatures Rise

My pot-bellied appearance makes me one of the chubbiest lizards around. Loose folds of skin hang around my neck and shoulders. I look like a smaller lizard trying to fit into its father's clothes!

Every morning I welcome the day by sunbathing on top of my favorite boulder. There I bask—all 16 inches of me—until my body temperature reaches a comfortable 100 to 105 degrees. That is when I begin my search for breakfast. I am 100 percent herbivorous, which means that I avoid meat. I hunt only for juicy desert plants—flowers, cactus fruit, leaves, and buds. God fashioned my body with special glands that help store water from the plants I eat. I also have a way to get rid of excess salt from the foods I eat: I sneeze!

He gave me a protective coat of armor, too—small scales all over my body. Larger scales guard my ear openings. Temperatures in the desert can change quickly from night to day. I can change, too. God taught me how to adjust my body colors from dark to light or from

light to dark, to help control my body temperature. If it's a hot day, I'll turn a lighter shade to reflect the sun. When it's chilly, my color will darken to absorb more heat.

God thought of everything when he created me—**Chuckwalla.**

More on the Web

Death Valley, California is home to a variety of lizards. Here are some photos of chuckwallas and friends:

http://cluster4.biosci.utexas.edu/deathvalley/Art/Polich.htm

Tell a Friend

Have you ever heard an angry person described as someone who is "hot under the collar"? When the chuckwalla's body temperature rises, it reflects the sun. Likewise, when we start to feel the heat of anger, we can turn to the Son—Jesus—for help. From the Bible passage below, we will learn how to control anger before it controls us.

Read About It

"Get rid of all hard feelings, anger and rage. Stop all fighting and lying. Put away every form of hatred. Be kind and tender to one another. Forgive each other, just as God forgave you because of what Christ has done."—Ephesians 4:31, 32

Lizards in Bible times scampered through king's palaces. Read about it in Proverbs 30:28.

Pray About It

I want to follow your example, Lord. When I start to feel "hot under the collar," help me to turn to you instead of lashing out.

The Snake That's Never Late

S nakes travel in different ways, just as people run, walk, skip, and jump. Some snakes crawl on the ground or side-wind on slippery surfaces where they can't get a good grip. Others swim, slither up trees, or burrow into holes in the ground. Not me! I am a flying snake!

I don't take off from a runway, and I don't depend on an air traffic controller to tell me where to fly. God gave me the ability to fly from one place to another, but I can't fly upward like an airplane or bird. I'm sometimes called a "parachuter," much like a flying squirrel. That means that I have to start my flight at a point that is higher than the place I want to land.

As I glide through the air, I hold my tail up higher than the rest of my body, and wag from side to side for balance. The outer edges of my belly scales are rigid, while the middle scales fold upwards. The angle of my scales acts like a parachute, slowing me down and prolonging my flight. I can travel over three times the length of a football field.

I live in the lowland tropical rainforests of southeast and south Asia. My home is in the trees there, so I am known as a tree snake. I have an appetite for small prey like lizards, frogs, birds, and bats.

God thought of everything when he created me—**Flying Tree Snake.**

More on the Web

More facts about flying tree snakes, plus pictures!

http://www.naturia.per.sg/buloh/verts/flying_tree_snake.htm

Tell a Friend

The flying tree snake takes shortcuts by flying from tree to tree. We sometimes do that, too. When you are tempted to hurry through an important task, remember this: God honors those who work hard to complete a task to the best of their ability.

Read About It

"Work at everything you do with all your heart. Work as if you were working for the Lord, not for human masters."—Colossians 3:23

Pray About It

Thank you for giving me important jobs to do, Lord. Remind me to do my very best for you, and to have a good attitude no matter what the task.

I have ridges on my belly that help me grip smooth surfaces.

Giant Bell of the Sea

I'm a giant of the Arctic seas! I'm an *invertebrate*, which means I have no spine. I don't have a heart, brain, blood, or gills, either. I don't even have eyes, but I do have organs that sense light from darkness.

My body is called a bell, because of its shape. It can reach a diameter of over eight feet! On the surface of my bell is an opening like a mouth. Frilly arms hang around it, helping me capture and eat small animals called *zooplankton*. I'm able to smell and taste, even though I don't have a nose or tongue!

Longer arms, called *tentacles*, hang down in eight clusters. My tentacles are 98 feet long—longer than a blue whale! They are armed with stinging cells. Inside each cell is a special hair that sends a danger signal to me when it detects any movement nearby. Like a harpoon flying toward my victim, I can fire off a painful sting in just a few milliseconds—less than a second! My sting injects a poison that

attacks the nerves of my victim.

I travel by riding the ocean currents and forcing water out of my bell to push myself around. God gave me a special way to stay upright: if my bell starts to tip, special nerves send a message to my muscles that tell them to tighten. That keeps me moving in the right direction.

God thought of everything when he created me—**Lion's Mane Jellyfish.**

More on the Web

The National Aquarium in Baltimore, Maryland has a giant jellyfish on display:

http://www.cnn.com/EARTH/9607/29/jellyfish/four.species.jpg

Tell a Friend

A jellyfish probably won't ever sting you, but stinging insults are hurtful, too. Choose your words carefully, because once you say them, it's impossible to take them back!

Read About It

"Lord, may the words of my mouth and the thoughts of my heart be pleasing in your eyes. You are my Rock and my Redeemer."—Psalm 19:14

I grow up to eight feet wide, 1000 feet long, and have up to 12,000 stinging tentacles!

Pray About It

Lord, help me to think before I speak and to choose words that bless, not hurt.

What a Laugh!

I hatched in a nest on top of a termite's mound in the woodlands of eastern Australia. It was a safe place for a home because predators didn't bother the eggs there.

You might recognize my loud call. My hysterical "laughter" often echoes through theaters whenever a movie includes a jungle scene. It's how I announce my territory, and it gives my family a unique way to communicate with each other, too.

I never drink, because my diet supplies all the moisture I need. I spend most of my day poised on high branches overlooking the rainforest. My vision is sharp, and I can spot my next meal in a hurry. I swoop down and grab frogs, lizards, large insects, mice, and snakes up to three feet long!

I am not in a rush to leave the nest, but stay with my family for about four years. During that time, my parents assign me the duty of incubating eggs and supplying nesting material to keep the nest nice

and cozy. You should hear us all laughing at once!

God thought of everything when he created me—**Laughing Kookaburra.**

More on the Web

"Kookaburra" has been popular children's song for generations. Listen to it here, then follow the link to a sound clip of a real laughing kookaburra!

http://www.calm.wa.gov.au/plants_animals/odd_kookaburra.html

Tell a Friend

The kookaburra uses its voice as a tool to communicate. Its "laughter" travels through the jungle like a message on a loudspeaker. What does your voice—and the way you use it—say about you?

Read About It

"Thoughtless words cut like a sword. But the tongue of wise people brings healing."—Proverbs 12:18

Here in Australia, our loud call is known as a "bushman's clock." God gave me an unusual voice, and I use it at dawn, midday, and dusk to celebrate the passing of a day.

Pray About It

Lord, I want my words to help, not hurt. Teach me to think before I speak, and to speak words that bless my friends and honor you.

Diving for Dinner

Before I hatched, my mother carried me in a bright orange egg sac. She sensed when it was time to build a nursery web around the egg case. She attached her bundle of eggs to a plant, and wrapped an extra web around it for support. I stayed in the spiderling nursery until I was strong enough to begin life on my own. Then I headed for the water.

I now live on the steep bank of a creek in Ecuador. God taught me how to dash across the surface of the water without sinking. The tension of the water's surface prevents me from going under. He gave me hairs on the tips of my legs that help me tread water. I move so fast, I don't break the surface of the water. Unsuspecting tadpoles, insects, frogs, and fish do not realize I'm there. When I detect vibrations below, I dive into the water and wrestle with a wriggling victim. Then I carry it to a quiet place on the water's edge, where I eat it all in

one sitting. Imagine that! I measure less than an inch, yet I'm able to capture a meal many times my size.

I have an appetite that doesn't seem to end. In fact, a scientist recorded one of my cousins eating not one, but *two* tadpoles within 24 hours. That would be like eating several large pizzas all by yourself!

God thought of everything when he created me—**Fishing Spider.**

More on the Web
Want to eyeball a close-up photo of me?

http://bugbios.com/entophiles/arthropoda/arth_en003.html

Tell a Friend
The fishing spider is small, yet mighty. No matter what age or size we are, God is able to use us exactly as we are. With God on our side, we can accomplish much! When we feel weak, we don't have to worry. God is a strong helper.

Read About It
"Look to the Lord and to his strength. Always look to him."
—Psalm 105:4

When I'm hungry, I brace my hind legs on a leaf or rock as I wait to spring into action. One silk strand anchors me to the shore like a lifeline, just in case I start to sink in the water.

Pray About It
Sometimes I feel too young or too small or too weak, Lord. Thanks for giving me your Word to remind me you are there to help me always.

A Furry Creature of Habit

If you were to spot me hopping through the snow, you might mistake me for a rabbit. But I'm much different than a common rabbit. Rabbits are born naked, with closed eyes. I was born covered with fur, with my eyes open. I could hop around almost from the time I was born.

I have unusually large, furry hind feet, which enable me to travel easily over snow. As I travel, I spread four long toes on each foot. That makes my feet even broader, like snowshoes. My Creator knew how easy it would be for predators to spot me moving along the white snow, so he planned a perfect way to protect me. In winter, my coat blends right in with the pure white of my surroundings. When warmer weather arrives, I begin shedding my fur, so that by summer my coat is a soft grayish brown. I blend in with every season!

I am a creature of habit. I travel back and forth between feeding and resting sites, using the same path every time. After several of my family members use it, the path looks like a snow-covered airport runway! By the time summer rolls around, we are so used to our route, we stick to it. If a plant blocks our trail, we just eat it!

God thought of everything when he created me—**Snowshoe Hare.**

More on the Web

More fun facts, plus a photo of a snowshoe hare!

http://www.northstar.k12.ak.us/schools/joy/creamers/Mammals/Studenthtmls/Hare/hare.html

Tell a Friend

The snowshoe hare sticks to the same path, no matter what the season. It is well traveled and takes him everywhere he needs to go. God promises to bless those who stay on track, according to his Word.

Read About It

"The path of those who do what is right is like the first gleam of dawn. It shines brighter and brighter until the full light of day."
—Proverbs 4:19

Pray About It

Lord, I want to be like the snowshoe hare, following the same path—your path—for all of my life.

Psalm 148 tells us that all of nature praises the Lord— even the snow beneath the feet of the snowshoe hare!

57

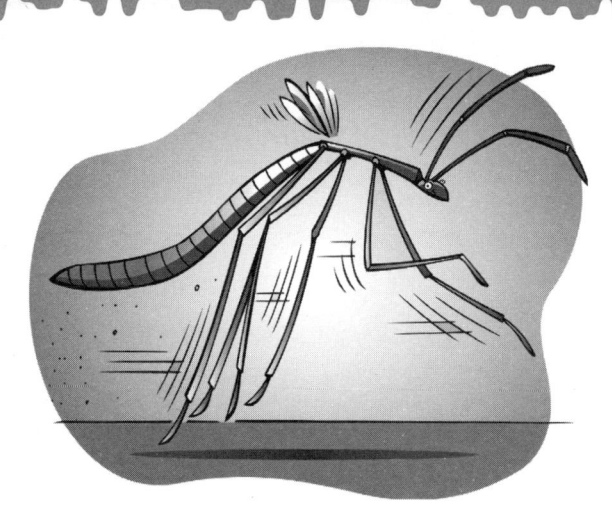

Stick 'em Up!

I began in an egg, where I developed for 12 to 16 months. One spring night, I hatched in the cool, damp soil under a clump of ferns. I pushed open my egg, climbed a nearby stem, and waited about 24 hours before I began my search for food.

I'm closely related to cockroaches, praying mantises, and grasshoppers. Females in my family grow wings, but are unable to fly. I am a male, and have the ability to fly if I need to. Because my wings are relatively small compared to my body size, scientists are stumped by how I can make it off the ground. I am over a foot long, but females of my species grow even longer!

In 1985, some of my cousins were chosen to travel on the D1 Spacelab mission, aboard a space shuttle! Experiments were carried out to study how low gravity and exposure to outer space would affect stick insect eggs.

Because I move so slowly, I'm not able to hurry down to a nearby

stream when I'm thirsty. God knew I'd have a problem getting water when I needed it, so he made my body with special blood that helps me conserve water for long periods of time

God thought of everything when he made me—**Giant African Stick Insect.**

More on the Web

Visit one of my South African cousins!

http://www.museums.org.za/bio/insects/phasmida/phalces_brevis.htm

Tell a Friend

God gave the giant African stick insect a special way to deal with thirst. Did you know that people feel spiritually thirsty without God? We need him just as a thirsty person needs water. Long before Jesus came, Scripture predicted our Savior's arrival. Read how Jesus was described in the passage below.

Read About It

"He will be like a place to hide from storms. He'll be like streams of water flowing in the desert. He'll be like the shadow of a huge rock in a dry and thirsty land."—Isaiah 32:2

My wings are unusually small for the size of my body, but that doesn't stop me from flying. Scientists call me a "one of the wonders of aerodynamics."

Pray About It

Dear God, thank you for sending Jesus to take away my spiritual thirst!

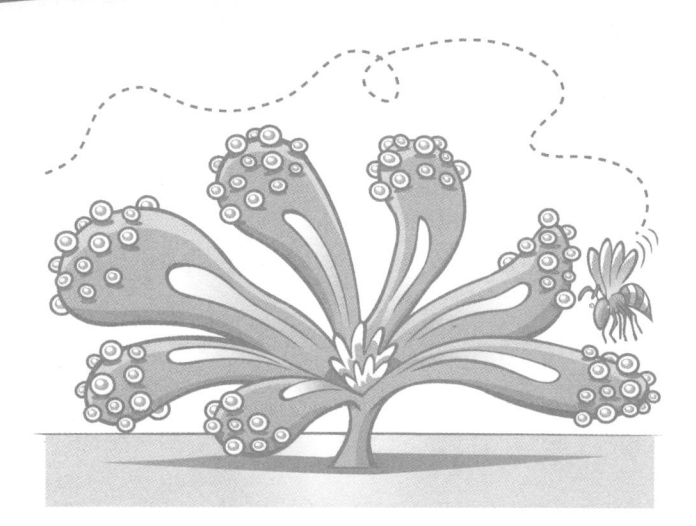

Today's Special:
Savory Insect Stew

I'm a hardy plant that lives in the desert country of western Australia, where moisture is available to me only during the winter months. Rather than sentencing me to bake all summer long without water, God came up with an excellent solution. I live underground as a bulb during the hot months of the year. When cooler fall and winter months arrive, I poke my head up through the soil and drink in the rain like a thirsty pup.

Here in the dry desert, soil lacks the nutrients I need, so God planned another way for me to get the goodies I need to grow. He covered my round-tipped leaves with tiny droplets that look like dew. Insects climb onto my leaves for a drink of water, and a honey-like substance entraps them.

Slowly my leaves fold around their wriggling bodies like a blan-

ket, soaking them in a digestive chemical. It's bug soup at its best!
After my meal, I uncurl my leaves again to get rid of any leftover
insect parts.

God thought of everything when he created me—**Sundew.**

More on the Web

Take a tour of a boggy home where some of my cousins live.

http://www.ipcc.ie/bogtour3.html

Tell a Friend

The sundew begins life with a single root. Without that taproot, it
could not establish itself solidly in the ground and grow. As believers
in Christ, we draw our nourishment from him. Read about how we
can grow spiritual roots.

Read About It

"You received Christ Jesus as Lord. So keep on living in him. Have
your roots in him. Build yourselves up in him. Grow strong in what you
believe, just as you were taught. Be more thankful than ever before."
—Colossians 2:6, 7

As a young plant, I grew a
taproot—a long root extending
deep underground. The taproot
delivered nutrients and moisture
to me for a year, until I grew
permanent roots that would
support me for the rest of my life.

Pray About It

Everything I am and everything I have is because of
you, Lord. Help me to depend
on you and follow you faith-
fully all the days of my life.

Find Me if You Can!

When October storms chase away most bird species in Canada's alpine passes, you won't see me packing my bags. Nope! I am among a few hardy birds that stay put throughout the winter. A member of the grouse family, I am equipped to survive even the coldest conditions.

God created me with feathered feet that keep me warm and help me to waddle across snow without sinking. I have a chunky body with short legs, small wings, and a stubby tail. I spend most of my time on the ground like a chicken, so my feathered feet are perfect!

Like many of my cold-weather friends, I have a special camouflage that protects me from predators during snowy months. My feathers change colors three times a year. After wearing white feathers for winter, I change into a covering of gold, brown, and black. By summer, most of my body has turned a chestnut brown. My change of "clothing" enables me to eat without fear of being attacked.

During winter, I feed by day and by night I roost in snow burrows—tunnels dug into the snow. I spend the winter nibbling seeds and buds of trees like birch, willow, and alder.

God thought of everything when he created me—**Ptarmigan.**

More on the Web

Read about a ptarmigan who lives in the Arctic.

http://www.mnh.si.edu/arctic/html/ptarmigen.html

Tell a Friend

God provides a protective covering for the ptarmigan. Christians have a protective covering, too. Ours is not made of feathers, but is a strong head-to-toe armor! Read about it in the Bible passage below.

Read About It

"Put the belt of truth around your waist. Put the armor of godliness on your chest. Wear on your feet what will prepare you to tell the good news of peace. Also, pick up the shield of faith. With it you can put out all of the flaming arrows of the evil one. Put on the helmet of salvation. And take the sword of the Holy Spirit. The sword is God's word."—Ephesians 6:14-17

Pray About It

Lord, you are my great protector. Thank you for equipping me from head to toe to live for you!

God gave me a keen sense for locating food, even when it's buried beneath snow.

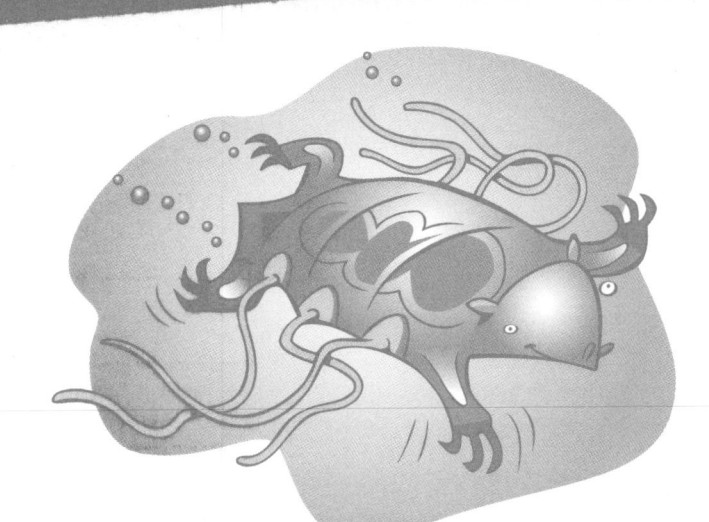

The Toughest Little Critter on Earth

My official name is *tardigrade*—a big name for a tiny creature like myself. I'm both tiny and transparent, and measure about one third of a millimeter long—about the size of the period at the end of this sentence. I'm a tiny freshwater animal with a short, plump body and four pairs of stumpy legs. Each leg has two-toed claws, which help me cling to plants. I dine on slimy algae and the plants upon which it lives. I lumber along like a miniature bear, stopping to picnic along the way.

You'll find me living in round, rain-soaked clumps of moss on shed roofs, gutters, or around ponds. Some of my relatives live at the base of trees, too. Don't expect to see me without the help of a microscope, though. Try soaking moss in water, then squeeze it dry. Drop some of the water on a glass slide and see how many of my family

members you can find.

If my home freezes in winter or bakes in summer until it's dry, God taught me an emergency plan. I simply pull my legs in, shrivel up, and roll into a tight ball until things return to normal. In fact, scientists found one of my cousins that had rolled itself up in a bottle of dried moss—for 120 years! When they added water, it perked right up.

God thought of everything when he created me—**Water Bear.**

More on the Web

Read an amazing fact about a water bear at the National Geographic website:

http://www.nationalgeographic.com/world/amfacts/amaz3.html

Tell a Friend

The water bear has a God-given emergency plan for tough times. So do we! God does not promise to spare us from problems, but he does promise to help us find a way through them.

Read About It

"The Lord saves those who do what is right. He is their place of safety when trouble comes."—Psalm 37:39

Pray About It

Dear God, help me not to shrink away when trouble comes, but to place my trust in you.

Scientists have tested my ability to survive tough conditions by exposing me to temperatures of 457 degrees below zero. I survived!

A Four-Inch Violin

If you were to visit the forests of Malaysia, you'd want to watch where you sit. You cannot just plop down on any old log or stump, because a sting from me could paralyze your fingers for 24 hours. God gave me a weapon to use in my defense—special glands that eject a fluid called *butyric acid*. He knew that I would need to be able to defend myself, even though I look creepy at four inches long.

I'm sometimes called a violin beetle, because my shape resembles the stringed musical instrument by that name. My wing covers extend out in large, flat flaps at each side of my body. My whole body is flat, almost as if someone squeezed the air out of me. My flattened shape allows me to sneak into small spaces where I would not otherwise be able to crawl, like crevices, cracks in the soil, and under bark.

In the humid forests of Malaysia, I creep along in those tiny spaces, in search of my next meal. Dinner usually consists of young insects. My head is longer than most beetles, which helps me to liter-

ally "stick my neck out" in my quest for food. It also helps me to peer into cracks and crevices before I enter.

God thought of everything when he created me—**Java Fiddle Beetle.**

More on the Web

How would you like to run into me in the forest?

http://coleoptera.chat.ru/Carabidae/Mormolyce.htm

Tell a Friend

God designed this beetle with a neck that helps it safely check out unknown territory before entering. In a similar way, the Bible tells us how to make wise decisions. God's Word will never steer us in the wrong direction!

Read About It

"God has breathed life into all of Scripture. It is useful for teaching us what is true. It is useful for correcting our mistakes. It is useful for making our lives whole again. It is useful for training us to do what is right."—2 Timothy 3:16

When my species was first discovered, insect collectors paid enormous prices for us. A good-looking beetle like me could sell for hundreds of dollars.

Pray About It

Dear Lord, your Word is like a long love letter to the world. Thank you for the way it helps me to know you better.

Mama Mía, It's a Mamba!

I began life in a warm, damp burrow in the ground. My mother laid over a dozen eggs there in my underground nest before deserting us. When the eggs hatched, we were already 16 to 24 inches long.

You'd better wear running shoes if you're going to travel with me. I travel 12 miles per hour—all 14 feet of me. I'm as long as an average male alligator! Members of my species live in pairs or small groups. I don't have to worry about predators, because nobody wants to mess with me. Before antivenin medication was developed, my bites were always fatal.

I have a reputation as the most deadly snake in the world! My body is a brownish-gray color and my back is brown and scaly. When I sense danger, I will raise my head and front body section four feet off the ground, open my mouth wide, and shake my head. I can strike from four to six feet away, and I'm usually accurate.

Once I strike a larger victim, I follow along while my poisonous

venom works its way through the animal's bloodstream. When my victim becomes paralyzed, I prepare for a feast. God gave me flexible jaws that make it possible for me to eat an animal in one piece!

God thought of everything when he created me—**Black Mamba.**

More on the Web

Adrian Warren spent several decades photographing images from nature. Here are some he took of this deadly snake:

http://www.lastrefuge.co.uk/images/html/reptiles/snakes/preview_html/snake01.html

Tell a Friend

At first glance, the black mamba does not look so deadly. In fact, it is a beautiful creature. Sin is like that; it wears a pretty disguise and tries to convince us that it can't hurt us. God will never trick us, though. He is always looking out for our good.

Read About It

"Watch and pray. Then you won't fall into sin when you are tempted. The spirit is willing. But the body is weak."—Matthew 26:41

When Jesus was preparing his 12 disciples to share the message of God's love he advised them to be wise like a snake See why in Matthew 10:16.

Pray About It

Dear Lord, give me strength and courage to make good choices. Help me to turn away from anything that would pull me away from your path.

Apartment for Rent

Everybody needs friends, and I am no exception. I'm a rainforest tree in South America, nicknamed an "ant tree," because the Azteca ant uses me as an apartment building. My branches and trunk are hollow, and are divided into a series of chambers by partitions. My partitions are like hallways, connecting all the "apartments."

God created me with a special oil and sugary substance on tiny leaf hairs, and at the base of each leaf. My oil and sugar nourish a certain type of ant—the Azteca.

When Azteca ants first arrive, the queen sets up a nest in a hollow chamber. Workers get busy in the other spare chambers until the entire tree becomes a colony of hard-working ants. The workers take what they need from me, but also protect me from insects and rainforest vines. The strangler fig, for example, would love to wrap its woody arms around my trunk and squeeze the life out of me. But it doesn't have a chance with Azteca ants on board.

When my dangling fruit ripens, it attracts many different animals. Its seeds are a popular treat for birds, rodents, and other rainforest creatures. The animals digest the seeds, then replant them naturally when they leave piles of waste in the forest. The process starts all over again—just as my Creator planned.

God thought of everything when he created me—**Cecropia Tree.**

More on the Web

Learn why the cecropia tree is an important part of the rainforest:

http://www.asij.ac.jp/elementary/projects/3-s/rainweb/cecropiause2.htm

Tell a Friend

Have you ever heard the saying, "To gain a friend, you must be a friend"? The cecropia tree is a friend to Azteca ants, and vice versa. They depend on each other for their very existence. Read below what the Bible says about the early church members, and how they supported each other.

Read About It

"All the believers were agreed in heart and mind. They didn't claim that anything they had was their own. They shared everything they owned."—Acts 4:32

Azteca ants benefit from a special partnership with the cecropia tree. Read what the Bible says about the way ants diligently work to gather food, in Proverbs 30:25.

Pray About It

Thank you for giving me such wonderful friends, Lord. Help me find ways to show them that I care.

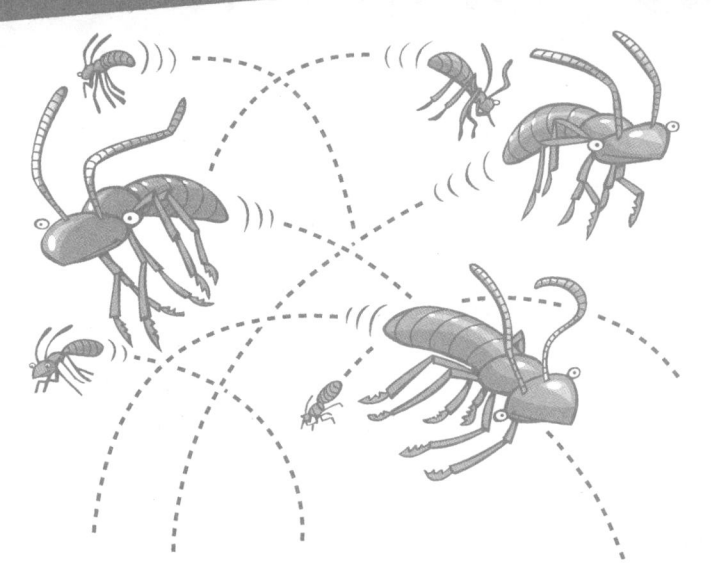

Flea on a Pogo Stick

I f you live in a snowy part of the world, you might have noticed a sprinkling of black flecks across your front yard. It looks as if someone peppered the snow. Those flecks are actually my friends and me—tiny insects that come out on sunny days to chomp away at decaying leaf litter. We hop around and eat like we're at a potluck dinner, and some people confuse us for fleas. Our favorite foods are goodies like bacteria, fungi, and algae on the snow's surface. As snow melts at the base of trees, we lunch on leaf litter.

My official name is *collembola*, but I'm sometimes referred to as a snow flea. I'm actually nothing like a flea, but you know how nicknames stick. God created me with two tails on my back end. Tucked underneath my belly, the tails are held snugly in place by tiny hooks. When I want to move, I unlatch my tails. They drop quickly, sending me shooting into the air. I look like a flea on an invisible pogo stick!

I don't feel the cold there on your snowy lawn, because my black

color absorbs sunshine. God takes good care of me while I work to help break down organic matter on the forest floor. You might call me a builder—a *soil* builder, that is. I digest plant litter, process it as waste, and return it to the soil.

God thought of everything when he created me—**Springtail.**

More on the Web

Have you ever seen this character in your yard?

http://www.nps.gov/olym/insect/colemb.htm

Tell a Friend

The springtail serves an important purpose. It may be tiny, but it has a job to do! Its work makes a big difference in our world. Don't wait until you grow up to make a difference. Find someone who needs help and ask God to show you ways to help him or her.

Read About It

"We work together with God. You are like God's field. You are like his building."—1 Corinthians 3:9

Pray About It

Lord, I want to make a difference in my world. Help me to share your love with those who are in need.

Did you know, the Bible mentions a flea in 1 Samuel 24:14?

73

Life Inside a Chimney

On the ocean floor off the coast of Mexico, the earth's crust is cracking and shifting. I am a four-inch worm that lives inside a formation on the ocean floor known as a *hydrothermal vent.* The vents are scattered about like small doors in the sides of underwater volcanoes. A geyser of boiling toxic water shoots upward through the vents.

I make my home in papery tubes that I burrow into the sides of the chimneys. Hot water from inside the vent flushes through my chimney home and flows into much colder deep-sea water outside. God taught me how to position my head in the cool area and my tail where it's hot. Just imagine what it would be like to have the heat running in your living room, and the air conditioner blowing cold air in the room next to it!

Scientists are baffled by my ability to adjust back and forth between temperatures without turning into worm stew. They suspect that my hairy shawl—a fuzzy coat of hair hanging from my back like a

fringed shawl—has something to do with it. They've gathered samples of my hair to study in special tests, and guess what? The hair contains proteins called *eurythermal* enzymes, which can stand all kinds of temperatures without being hurt! Scientists are hoping to learn more, and think that someday the proteins from my shawl will help them create new and better products like medicines, paper, detergents, and textiles.

God thought of everything when he created me—**Pompeii Worm.**

More on the Web

I posed for a portrait so you could see my fuzzy bacterial coat. Aren't I handsome?

http://dsc.discovery.com/news/briefs/20010220/bugs_zoom.html

Tell a Friend

Just as God prepared the Pompeii worm to tolerate intense heat, so he can help you in times of trouble. If you've ever had a "heated" argument with a friend, you know how bad it made you feel afterwards. God has good advice for controlling hot tempers in the verse below.

Read About It

"A gentle answer turns anger away. But mean words stir up anger."
—Proverbs 15:1

There are thousands of different species of worms in the world. The Bible mentions one type in Job 7:5.

Pray About It

Lord, I know that a hot-tempered argument can damage a good friendship.

My Messy Claim to Fame

Mention the name *packrat*, and eyebrows will raise. A packrat is usually somebody who has a hard time parting with stuff. I earned the nickname because my most memorable trait is the way I build a *midden* and keep adding to it my entire life. A midden is an ever-growing heap of garbage, and a "bathroom" area for critters like me.

Sometimes a midden is built apart from a nesting area, but occasionally, members of my species feel so attached to their midden, they'll move into the heap and raise their babies there. That's exactly what I've chosen to do. To keep the pile from caving in on us, I glue my collection together with urine. The sun turns my urine into crystals, which holds the whole heap together. It's a way to mark my property, just as if I'd hung a sign that says, "Keep out!" on the doorway of my home. Scientists have found ancient middens still glued together after thousands of years, which allows them to study the living habits of my ancestors.

Besides my midden, I build several food piles to last all through the winter. I don't hibernate, so my food needs are the same year round. And speaking of food needs—I am a favorite food of owls! Researchers have decided that I stick close to home for fear of being hunted down and eaten. What do you think?

God thought of everything when he created me—**White-Throated Woodrat.**

More on the Web

Look at this fossilized midden, discovered in a cave in the Grand Canyon!

http://www.usgs.nau.edu/methods/images/crystal.gif

Tell a Friend

A white-throated woodrat keeps everything. It builds its heap higher and higher as a way of saying, "This is my territory, so back off!" Do you surround yourself with material things instead of people? Are you missing some good friendships, or maybe special times with the Lord, because material things take up so much of your time?

Read About It

"You open your hand and satisfy the needs of every living creature."

—Psalm 145:16

When seeking food for babies, the females of my species wander as far away as 984 feet—more than three times the length of a football field.

Pray About It

Dear God, help me to enjoy the things I own, without letting them own me.

Hairy Ol' What's-His-Name

I'm a critter with many nicknames. Some call me *sun scorpion*, even though I'm not a scorpion at all. Scorpions love sunshine, but I prefer to wander only at night. I am called *wind scorpion* because I look like I'm running as fast as the wind. Still others refer to me as *sun spider* because I make my home in sunny desert areas.

I belong to the family of *arachnids*—otherwise known as spiders. Worldwide, my family has 800 to 900 different species. In North America, there are almost 120 different types of arachnids. Imagine if we all showed up at your door!

If you run into me, it will most likely be at night—and I guarantee you won't forget me. God gave me four pairs of legs, but I use only three pairs to run. While scampering across the ground, I hold up my front legs and use them like a set of antennae. My bulky body is covered with hair, and my long legs span almost six inches! I am attracted to light, which is less than happy news to anyone reading by flash-

light in a tent! Although I have a terrible reputation as a fierce biter, relax—I'm not poisonous.

Since I am not a hopping spider or a web-swinging spider, I rely on my speed and skill to hunt down and catch my prey. My favorite midnight snack is termites, but I'll settle for a nice juicy lizard, a grasshopper, or a crunchy beetle.

God thought of everything when he created me—**Camel Spider.**

More on the Web

I posed for this photo during one of my hunts:

http://www.sasionline.org/arthzoo/solpgd.htm

Tell a Friend

The camel spider moves naturally toward light. So do people—except our light is Jesus. Read how his light changes lives for the better, both now and forever.

God's Word speaks of a man named John the Baptist who wore camel-hair clothes and ate locusts and honey. Read about him in Matthew 3:1-6.

Read About It

"I have come into the world to be a light. No one who believes in me will stay in darkness."—John 12:46

Pray About It

Heavenly Father, help me to share your light with my friends so that they can experience your great love.

No Lily Pads for Me!

Move over, Spider-Man! I have extra-long toes, complete with toe pads to help me stick snugly to vertical surfaces. My huge webbed hands and feet make it possible for me to glide through the air like a bird. I simply spread my toes, take a leap—and I'm off! God designed my hind legs larger than the legs in front because he knew I would need to push off when I leap from a branch. When spread fully, my webbed feet catch the air like a wind sail on a boat. I can glide easily for 50 feet.

My moist tropical home provides me with endless flights from tree to tree. I have a beautiful view up from my treetop, too—a bright green rainforest canopy stretched out for as far as I can see. My back and legs glow a shiny green color in contrast to the undersides and in-between sections of my toes, which are a striking yellow. My body is only four inches long, but when I soar from tree to tree with my yellow sails, I measure one square foot!

Extra flaps of skin along both sides act as a built-in air control tool. As I near my target, special bones press firmly against my toes, readying my toe pads to grab onto the side of a tree trunk.

God thought of everything when he created me—**Wallace's Flying Frog.**

More on the Web

Here is a photo of me resting after a giddy glide.

http://www.accessexcellence.org/21st/TL/sly/sly_imgWin21.html

Tell a Friend

God thoughtfully prepared Wallace's flying frog with all it needs for flying. He cares for it from the time it pushes off a tree branch, to the moment its toe pads grab a tree trunk far below. God is busy preparing and equipping you for what he wants you to do with your life, too.

Read About It

"God's power has given us everything we need to lead a godly life."
—2 Peter 1:3

The Old Testament describes a time when frogs invaded the land of Egypt. Read about it in Exodus 8:1-15.

Pray About It

Dear Lord, help me to have the faith to turn loose of my doubts and fears and follow your perfect plan for my life.

A Sweet Termite Trap

I'm a reddish-colored plant from the tropical forests of Borneo. God designed me with hollow-tubed growths at the end of my leaves, called pitchers. The upper edge of each pitcher is decorated with a white ring of tiny hairs, which provides sweet, nourishing nectar. One type of termite is drawn to the hairs and seems unable to resist. The rim of each pitcher is covered with slippery wax, and the pitcher itself is filled with digestive fluid. As they feed, termites slip down the opening of my pitchers and cannot get out. Then it's time for *me* to feed as I start to digest the termites—yum!

During one experiment, scientists placed pitcher plants across the path of some traveling termites. Sure enough, up to 22 termites per minute crawled up the plant, ate the hairs, and were soon trapped inside. Researchers peered inside and found thousands of termites from the same species trapped there. Once the hairs had been eaten, termites were no longer attracted to the plant.

Adult termites use my nectar for quick energy. Some manage to return home with nectar for their young, who need it to grow. I owe a lot to the tiny creatures that visit me—and to my Creator, who feeds me daily with a steady stream of termites.

God thought of everything when he created me—**Pitcher Plant.**

More on the Web

Look at these hungry termites marching up a pitcher plant:

http://dsc.discovery.com/news/reu/20011231/plant.html#

Tell a Friend

Termites are drawn to me by something that promises sweet refreshment. Sin is like that, too. It lures us to the "edge" with promises that it doesn't deliver. The good news is that we can resist temptation by turning to God for help.

Read About It

"You are tempted in the same way all other human beings are. God is faithful. He will not let you be tempted any more than you can take. But when you are tempted, God will give you a way out so that you can stand up under it."—1 Corinthians 10:13

Pray About It

Lord, it's great to know that I can call on you anytime and anywhere. Thank you for being my helper and friend.

God designed me to attract my prey with color, sugar, and smell.

When Life Turns Shifty

I can hop faster than a person can run. A single leap will carry me more than six feet! Can you top that?

At first glance, people often compare me to a gerbil, but I belong to a different family that is known for its remarkable jumping ability. My hind legs are four times longer than my front legs! I'm a silky, furry rodent with tan fur. My black tail tuft and facemask give me an air of mystery. If you picture me the size of a hopping kangaroo, think again. I am only three inches long!

Members of my species live in desert regions of Africa and Asia. God knew I'd need extra help, so he designed my feet with tufts of bristly hairs under my toes and on the soles of my hind feet. The hairs help me to grip the loose sand. It's useful for kicking sand behind me when I dig a burrow, too. God designed my ears with a tuft of protective hair, which keeps sand from blowing into my ear canal. Wasn't that thoughtful of my Creator?

I may look cute, but I don't like to be handled. If disturbed, I growl, shriek, and thump my back feet. Otherwise, I'm a quiet loner.

God thought of everything when he created me—**Jerboa.**

More on the Web

More facts about jerboa, plus an interactive paint box for painting its picture online.

http://www.enchantedlearning.com/cgi-bin/paint/faaLCrf/subjects/mammals/rodent/Jerboa.shtml

Tell a Friend

Jerboa gets a good grip on the loose desert sand, thanks to special footpads. God's Word helps us "get a grip," too, when we need extra encouragement in our life. His promises never grow old!

Read About It

"Give praise to the Lord. Give praise to God our Savior. He carries our heavy loads day after day."—Psalm 68:19

Pray About It

Lord, thank you for loving me so much! When I need encouragement, you are always there.

In the late spring and summer, I plug my burrow to air-condition my underground home. It keeps the heat out and the moisture inside.

Take Two Mandibles and Call Me in the Morning

I belong to a group of hunter ants that move along the forest floor in a fan-shaped swarm. We attack scorpions, tarantulas, roaches, beetles, grasshoppers, and adult ants of other tribes. It does not take long for us to wipe out the food supplies of an entire forest area.

The queen of my colony can produce 100,000 to 300,000 eggs in a span of 10 days. When it's time for our colony to move again, we all work together like backpackers to help carry the babies, called *larvae*, to the new campsite.

We are helpful to local rainforest peoples and to certain insects. Local natives place one of us over a skin wound. The ant reacts by clamping down with its strong jaws, called *mandibles*, which naturally close the skin like a doctor's stitch. Then they twist off the head of the ant, leaving the mandibles clamped tightly across the wound!

Wasps, millipedes, and beetles often sneak into our ranks, spraying the pathway with a chemical that copies our scent. Our eyesight is so poor, we don't notice that they've joined our march. They benefit by eating meals that have been captured by our workers.

God thought of everything when he created me—**South American Army Ant.**

More on the Web

Learn more about my hunting habits:

http://library.thinkquest.org/J0112365/insect/army_ant.htm?tqskip1=1&tqtime=0404

Tell a Friend

It's easy to pretend to be someone we're not—just as the insects do when they mimic the army ants. God sees into our hearts, though. He knows who we *really* are inside because he has known us since before we were born. Are you allowing God to help you become the person he created you to be?

Read About It

"God, see what is in my heart. Know what is there. Put me to the test. Know what I'm thinking. See if there's anything in my life you don't like. Help me live in the way that is always right."—Psalm 139:23, 24

Proverbs 6:6-8 uses me as an example of hard work and cooperation.

Pray About It

Dear God, help me discover who I am and who I can become with your help.

Guess Who's Coming for Dinner?

I live in the desert of the southwestern United States, where my enemies are few. I am an egg-bearing female wasp, and must find a tarantula in which to lay a single egg. To me, a tarantula is like a snug, warm baby nursery. God gave me a keen sense of smell to locate the spider's burrow.

Entering the burrow is not as easy as you might think! Tarantulas line their homes with silk, and stretch a silken trip wire outside the entrance as a gate. If an enemy wanders near, it jiggles the trip wire like a doorbell announcing a visitor. I love jiggling those trip wires, because it lures the spider out of its shelter in a hurry.

I poke at the tarantula with my antennae, until it rears up in a fighting position. We wrestle until I am able to maneuver in for a sting to its tender underside. I don't want to kill it, because I need a live

victim in order to carry out my plan. My poisonous sting paralyzes the hairy beast, but by the end of my attack, I am exhausted! I then probe the tarantula's open sting area and sip a "spider shake" from the fluids oozing there.

After that high-energy snack, I drag the hairy beast's body back inside its burrow, where I lay a single egg on its back. My egg eventually hatches into a baby grub, and feeds off the tarantula's body.

God thought of everything when he created me—**Tarantula Hawk.**

More on the Web

Learn more about this colorful black and red wasp at the Mojave National Preserve's website:

http://www.nps.gov/moja/mojaantw.htm

Tell a Friend

God gave tarantula hawk a clear sense of how and where to lay its egg. If it ignores that plan, its efforts will not succeed. How well do you listen to God? When you sense that you are making a foolish decision, do you back off, or stubbornly proceed?

Read About It

"Increase my knowledge and give me good sense, because I believe in your commands."—Psalm 119:66

A tarantula has nothing to fear from males of my species, since they don't have a stinger.

Pray About It

Forgive me for the times I stubbornly want my own way, Lord. Help me to listen instead of rushing ahead of you.

A Hard Nut to Crack

Over 300 years ago, I was part of a lush tropical forest on an island in the Indian Ocean. I am a strong hardwood tree that island residents used as their main source of timber. In the early 1970s, a scientist noticed that I had grown old and sickly. He found only about a dozen trees of my species still alive on the island, each over 300 years old. Although we were still producing seeds, none of our seeds would sprout into new trees.

A hard-shelled outer casing protects my seeds. My seeds are so hard, they require a special process in order to sprout. They must pass through the digestive tract of an animal with a special stomach, called a *gizzard*, that grinds hard-to-digest food.

Centuries ago, the flightless dodo bird used to feast on my fruit. The seeds would pass through the dodo's digestive tract, and they ended up growing wherever he deposited a pile of waste. Over the years, hunters who visited my island killed so many dodo birds that

they soon became extinct. Since no other animal ate my seeds, I was not able to produce new trees.

Scientists have been working hard to help my family of trees spread and grow again. They've discovered new ways to crack and grow my hard-shelled seeds with the help of wild turkeys. They hope that someday the island of Mauritius will once again enjoy a lush forest full of my hardwood trees.

God thought of everything when he created me—**Calvaria Tree.**

More on the Web

Here's a detailed illustration of a dodo bird.

http://www.davidreilly.com/dodo/images/gallery/DODO1.jpg

Tell a Friend

God has equipped certain plants and animals for special tasks. Life goes smoothly for them when they work together. God also equips people to help and encourage others. Have you thought about how God could use your talents and abilities to help other people?

God planned for certain plants and animals to help each other. Scientists call such a partnership a SYMBIOTIC relationship.

Read About It

"Teach me to do what you want, because you are my God. May your good Spirit lead me on a level path."—Psalm 143:10

Pray About It

My friends are a special part of my life, Lord. Help me to serve and encourage my friends when they are in need.

My Glow-in-the-Dark Weapon

Life in the midwater ocean is cold and dark. Midwater is an area where sunlight cannot break through. At a depth of about 450 feet, light is either scattered or absorbed by the water. I live even deeper than that—about 1,300 to 3,500 feet below the ocean's surface. My brilliant red color appears black in the dim light of the midwater. God knew what he was doing when he painted me red. It's serves as a special camouflage!

Some of my shrimp cousins have been found living inside the shells of crabs, but not me. I like my freedom, so I swim in a large swarm. I look similar to a shrimp, except I have a deeper red color. I don't have to search very far for nourishment, because I like to feed on small particles of food that are left behind by fish that were too full to finish their meal. I'm about four inches long, but word has it that

one of my relatives grew to be over a foot long! As an important member of the ocean world, I help process waste and provide food for young fish during the winter.

I am considered a delicacy by many fish and seadragons. But guess what? God gave me a secret weapon to use when trouble comes near. If a predator starts to bother me, I spit out a special glow-in-the-dark fluid. My "flashlight" startles them and gives me time to escape!

God thought of everything when he created me—**Giant Red Mysid.**

More on the Web

Do you ever wear red? I do—every single day! Here's proof:

http://www.mbayaq.org/efc/living_species/default.asp?hOri=1&inhab=179

Tell a Friend

God planned a way of escape for the giant red mysid, and he will do the same for you. The mysid uses a special light as its secret weapon. God supplies believers with a powerful light through the Bible.

Read About It

"When your words are made clear, they bring light."—Psalm 119:130

More than 1,000 types of mysids live in the waters of the world. My species has an armored shell covered with spikes that discourage hungry predators.

Pray About It

Dear God, it is good to know that I can call on you in times of need. Thank you for always being there for me and lighting up my life with your love.

A Recipe for Trouble: Bounce, Shriek, and Run!

I'm a primate from the grasslands of Africa—a ground-dwelling monkey that avoids densely wooded areas. Scientists call me an *omnivore* because I eat whatever is available. I love to dine on pods, seeds, leaves, fruits, insects, eggs, lizards, and flowers of blooming trees.

Here in our family, called a *troop*, the highest-ranking female is in charge, while males guard our territory. As a male, I spend most of my time perched high in a tree or atop a cliff. I watch out for leopards, cheetahs, eagles, hyenas, and jackals. If a predator wanders too close, I start bouncing on a tree limb or bush. Making a lot of racket gives the rest of the troop time to sneak away or hide in the long grass. After the excitement dies down, we relax by leaning back and putting our feet up.

God colored my coat so that it perfectly blends in with the savanna grasses. It's mostly reddish-brown, but the underside of my body is white or gray. I sport a long mane of hair around my neck and shoulders, and a white mustache.

God designed my body with long, slender arms and legs. If I'm threatened, I can run up to 35 miles per hour, which is the speed limit in most cities and towns!

God thought of everything when he created me—**Patas Monkey.**

More on the Web

Sierra Safari Zoo has a patas monkey named Baby:

http://www.sierrasafarizoo.com/animals/patasmonkey.htm

Tell a Friend

The patas monkey knows what to do when it feels threatened: bounce, shriek, and run away. But we don't have to run away when problems come along. We can stand our ground and let God fight our battle for us.

Read About It

"When I am afraid, I will trust in you." —Psalm 56:3

Pray About It

Lord, it's nice to know that I don't have to run away from problems. Thank you for being my protector, my helper, and my Savior.

We're usually quiet, but our troop will bark when meeting another troop along a path.

Mighty Mouth of Madagascar

Mention my name and people shudder. Nobody likes me. That's because I remind them of a certain insect that is viewed as a filthy pest. You see, I am a member of the cockroach family. But not all roaches are created equal, and I don't look or behave like that dirty roach that scampers for cover near a garbage can.

I live on the damp forest floor in Madagascar, an island off the southeast coast of Africa. Since I am a cold-blooded insect, my body temperature adjusts itself to the temperature of my surroundings. I'm four inches long and I weigh almost as much as two sticks of butter!

I am definitely not an ordinary roach. For one thing, I don't stink, and neither do my droppings. I don't have wings or wing pads. I'm chocolate brown with dark orange marks on my abdomen. During the day, I hide under debris while I wait for nightfall. If I'm bothered, I'll

let loose with a hiss that is meant to scare off intruders. My signal alerts the other members of my colony who quickly join in. Sometimes we hiss just for the sake of hissing, like a choir warming up for its opening song.

God thought of everything when he created me—**Madagascar Hissing Cockroach.**

More on the Web

Check out this great picture of me:

http://senecaparkzoo.org/animals/reptiles/hissing_cockroach.jpg

Tell a Friend

The hissing cockroach's body adjusts to the temperature of its sur-roundings. When the temperature is hot, it heats up. When a cold wind blows, its body cools down. Make sure that outside influences—like certain friendships—don't dampen your relationship with God. Stand up for what you believe, no matter what other people think.

Read About It

"Lord, may the words of my mouth and the thoughts of my heart be pleasing in your eyes. You are my Rock and my Redeemer."
—Psalm 19:14

Some people keep me as an exotic pet. I thrive off of dog biscuits, lettuce, and celery.

Pray About It

Dear God, I want to walk close to you, no matter what everyone else does.

Orange-Eyed Night Stalker

I'm a giant among my species and the largest owl in Europe, with a wingspan of six feet! Females weigh almost nine pounds. My scientific name is *bubo bubo.* How would you like to go through life with a name like that?

God specially designed my feathers to be speckled with brown and black. He knew that I'd need plenty of camouflage during the day so I could rest without being bothered by predators. I sleep by day and hunt all night.

My ears are located on the side of my face. One of my ears sits a little higher than the other one so I can locate the exact direction of a sound! God molded a feather pattern around my eyes to form a dish shape. It works like a funnel, carrying sound into my ears. My eyes are a beautiful shade of orange, and I have perfect vision. With eyes

and ears working together, I'm sure to have a good night's hunt.

My partner and I met during a mating season, then built a nest together. We will stay together for life. Favorite nest sites for birds of my type include a cliff, rock crevice, or behind a bush on the ground. Some of us choose a nest that another large bird has abandoned.

God thought of everything when he created me—**Eagle Owl.**

More on the Web

Learn about my cousins, the North American owls, and listen to their calls!

http://www.owlpages.com/n_american_owls.html

Tell a Friend

The eagle owl has an unusual scientific name—*bubo bubo*. How do you feel about your name? Did you know that when somebody asks Jesus into their heart and life, he gives them a brand new name? Wearing the name "Christian" is a giant responsibility, because others will judge Jesus by the way we live and act.

Read About It

"Dear children, don't just talk about love. Put your love into action. Then it will truly be love."—1 John 3:18

The male eagle owl prepares several nest sites, then advertises them by clucking loudly. The female then tours each site and selects one as their home.

Pray About It

Lord, I want to make a difference in this world. Show me everyday ways I can share your love with others and bring honor to your name.

Welcome to the Hotel Amazonica

I'm an extraordinary plant with floating leaves that measure up to seven feet across—more than the height of an average man! I'm at home in the warm waters of South American lakes and rivers.

God created a partnership between a certain Amazon beetle and me. The beetle is attracted to my bright white flowers, which measure a full foot across and smell like a butterscotch and pineapple dessert. The blossoms open wide at night to provide a cozy 98-degree room for my insect friend. Inside my petal hotel, this large brown beetle feasts on sugars and starches.

The petals close as the flower cools, tucking the hungry beetle in for a cozy sleepover. God arranged for my flower to release pollen at dusk. When my flower opens up the next morning to release the beetle, it flies away with its body covered with pollen! As the beetle

searches for a new food supply, my pollen drops onto other flowers.

Once a flower has been pollinated, it sinks underwater and forms a seed-filled pod. The new seeds eventually float to the surface, where water carries them along to a spot where they will begin a new plant. Then the cycle will begin all over again, just as God planned.

God thought of everything when he created me—**Victoria Amazonica.**

More on the Web

Wow! Look at the underside of this huge leaf from a Victoria amazonica!

http://www.junglephotos.com/plants/waterplants/undrlily.html

Tell a Friend

God schedules meetings between beetles and the Victoria amazonica, and he plans special meetings in our lives, too. Think of friends he has brought across your path. Ask God how you can touch their lives with his love.

Read About It

"Lord, I will praise you among the nations. I will sing about you among the people of the earth. Great is your love. It is higher than the heavens. Your truth reaches to the skies."
—Psalm 108:3, 4

Named in honor of Queen Victoria of England in 1838, Victoria amazonica is the largest water lily in the world.

Pray About It

Thank you for the friends you have given me, Lord. Help my friendships to grow and show me ways to share your love with others.

Anteater of the Air

I live in Indonesia, where I feed on ants and termites. I'm an eight-inch lizard that is often compared to a hang glider. While some people occasionally hang glide for fun, it's how I travel every day! God outfitted me with over a dozen ribs connected by flat folds of skin. When I spread my "wings" and push off from a branch high above the forest, I sail majestically through the air for more than 150 feet—three times the width of a basketball court!

I'm a beautiful sight as I soar across the rainforest—a mixture of green, blue, and yellow-orange. If I fold my wings tightly against my sides, I blend in perfectly with my surroundings. I rarely touch the ground, because the ants that I eat live in the trees with me. When I'm hungry, I hang on the side of a tree trunk, waiting for ants to come close enough to grab without moving. Researchers have called me a "sit-and-wait feeder."

Every day between 11 a.m. and 1 p.m. I take a break from my

normal gliding and feeding activities. By doing so, I avoid the hottest hours of the day. I never glide when it's windy or raining, either. If a predator is hot on my trail, I automatically start climbing the nearest tree.

God thought of everything when he created me—**Flying Dragon Lizard.**

More on the Web

Get better acquainted with the flying dragon lizard:

http://centralpets.com/pages/critterpages/reptiles/lizards/LZD2644.shtml

Tell a Friend

Think of a time when you wished you could just soar above your problems, rather than solving them. Did you ask God for help? If not, why not?

Read About It

"Think about the ravens. They don't plant or gather crops. They don't have any storerooms at all. But God feeds them. You are worth much more than birds! Can you add even one hour to your life by worrying?"—Luke 12:24, 25

The Bible says that when we trust in God, he will give us strength when we're weary and help us to soar like eagles. See Isaiah 40:31.

Pray About It

Lord, you help me to rise above my problems. Thank you for teaching me to let go and trust you completely.

Hoses and Gaskets and Wiring, Oh My!

I live in the alpine region of New Zealand, where my family of parrots has a reputation for being extremely curious. We are unafraid of people and new environments. In the mid-1800s, our curiosity got us into big trouble. We were attacking sheep with our sharp curved beaks, which caused bacteria to enter their bloodstream through their wounds. Farmers hired hunters to kills us, and close to 150,000 parrots were shot. Today, our population only amounts to a few thousand parrots.

God created me in shades of green, blue, yellow, and red. I have a curved bill that acts like a set of portable tongs, making it easy for me to collect seeds, rootlets, insects, and larvae. I attract crowds and have been called "the clown of New Zealand's southern Alps." But tourists don't think I'm so funny when they discover that I've eaten

the rubber strips on their windshield wipers!

There's no end to my pranks. I like to roll stones down the iron roofs of mountain huts and steal the contents of backpacks. I can shred hiking boots in a short time, and love stealing sunglasses.

I'll never win a popularity contest, but I'm still considered one of the world's most intelligent, beautiful, and curious birds.

God thought of everything when he created me—**Kea.**

More on the Web

Learn more about this curious parrot at this New Zealand website.

http://www.learnz.org.nz/2002/aoraki/kea.htm

Tell a Friend

Sin can be a heavy burden until we face it and ask God for forgiveness. Don't be like the kea, who "plays dead" when he's caught. Admit your sin, turn away from wrong behavior, and ask for God's forgiveness.

Read About It

"Then I admitted my sin to you. I didn't cover up the wrong I had done. I said, 'I will admit my lawless acts to the Lord.' And you forgave the guilt of my sin."—Psalm 32:5

Members of my parrot family have been known to steal keys and then play dead when their deed is discovered.

Pray About It

Heavenly Father, thank you for lifting the guilt of my sin. Teach me good judgment, so I can make choices that honor you.

Mini-Hippo, Pig, or Deer?

My strange appearance would give a dentist nightmares! God gave me special teeth, called *tusks*, that actually look more like antlers. Instead of growing out of my mouth, my canine teeth grow through the upper part of my snout. They curve upward and back against my head. Although they look threatening, they're actually rather brittle and can break easily.

My family lives in small groups in the rainforest. Most of us are around three to four feet long, with a foot-long tail. I tip the scales at 200 pounds. I have a pudgy body, bristly skin, long snout, and small ears. My long, skinny legs speed me along to my favorite wallowing hole where I spend hours trying to rid my skin of parasites.

Mothers in my family build a soft, grassy nest for their babies. They give birth to only one or two babies at a time. Our lifestyle provides plenty of playmates for the young of our family, and helps us band together to watch out for predators. Trails connect our territory,

almost like sidewalks connecting a neighborhood. We visit each other often, like friendly neighbors or cousins.

By day, we are excellent runners and swimmers, which has helped our species establish new colonies from island to island along the coast of southeast Asia. At night, my family and I graze on grasses and feed on fruits, bugs, leaves, and water plants.

God thought of everything when he created me—**Babirusa.**

More on the Web

Here's a photo of an adult male member of my family:

http://www.stlzoo.org/content.asp?page_name=Babirusa

Tell a Friend

Babirusa appears to be a pig, yet has characteristics that make animal experts wonder about its identity. Christians take on a new identity when they ask Jesus into their hearts. When we allow his love to shine through us, others will notice a difference.

Read About It

"Anyone who believes in Christ is a new creation. The old is gone! The new has come!"—2 Corinthians 5:17

I communicate with a low grunt or a moan. When I'm excited, I clatter my teeth.

Pray About It

Lord, help me to live for you so others will notice my true identity as a follower of Jesus.

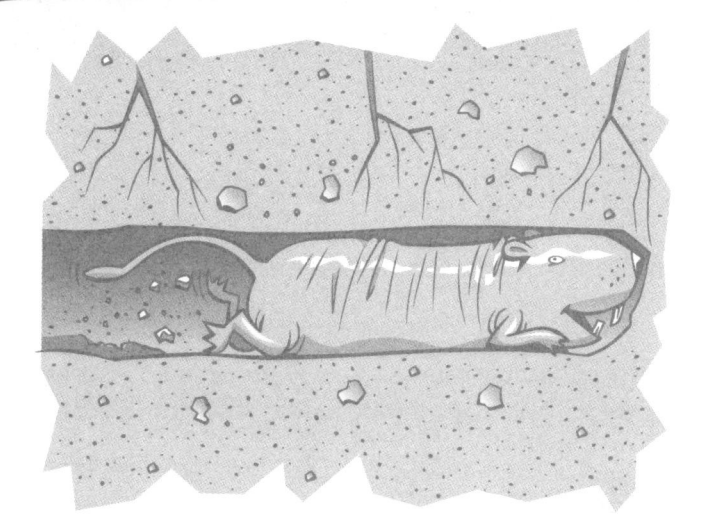

A Naked Tunnel Digger

I'm a small rodent with hair so fine and pale, it barely shows. Two teeth hang out of my mouth like mini tusks. I've been nicknamed a "hotdog with teeth."

Here in the hot, dry region of Africa, our family structure is often compared to that of ants and other insects. We have a queen, soldiers, and workers, and each group is responsible for certain tasks. We work hard, cooperating with each other to get the job done. Cooperation makes life run smoothly down in our burrow home.

God knew all along that I would be a tunnel-digger. He prepared me for that job by giving me a strong jaw muscle. It is considered the strongest jaw of any mammal my size. God also knew that I would need a way to keep dirt out of my mouth while digging. He attached extra folds of skin to both sides of my mouth to carry dirt away from my face like a drainpipe.

My home is an underground freeway system with tunnels that

lead to various rooms. It has a feeding room where we share our roots and tubers, and a nesting area where we sleep. We all lie in a big heap for warmth.

We can't smell anything, so if a newcomer from another colony enters our home, we accept him as one of our own. As far as we are concerned, if he looks like us, we must be related. We welcome him and put him to work.

God thought of everything when he created me—**Naked Mole Rat.**

More on the Web

Here's a detailed picture of me, plus fun facts about my life.

http://www.enchantedlearning.com/subjects/mammals/rodent/Nakedmolerat.shtml

Tell a Friend

Each member of naked mole rat's colony does its job without grumbling. So should we! If you rake yards, rake to the best of your ability. If you wash dishes, find a way to make it fun. When everyone pulls together and does a good job, a home runs smoothly.

I live in a colony of 20 to 300 individuals. Our family structure and work habits are similar to that of bees, wasps, ants, and termites.

Read About It

"All hard work pays off. But if all you do is talk, you will be poor."—Proverbs 14:23

Pray About It

Dear God, thank you for giving me work to do and for equipping me to do my best.

Hold the Mayo, I'm Not a Tomato!

On the east coast of Africa lies a place called Madagascar. It was there, on the surface of a swamp, my mother laid over 1,000 tiny eggs. Within two days, I hatched as a tadpole. Then about 45 days later, I changed into the cutest little froglet Mom had ever seen.

I am now the color of a vine-ripened tomato. It took several months for me to reach this brilliant orange-red color. Every now and then, if the humidity and temperature is not to my liking, my pretty coloration changes to a drab brown.

Males of my species grow to be two and a half inches long, but we females are larger. I measure almost four inches long and have a hearty appetite. I am what scientists call an "ambush hunter." At night, I sit and wait until my prey comes along, then I spring forward to catch my dinner. I will eat just about anything that moves, including

flies, moths, crickets, mealworms, worms, and grasshoppers.

God designed my head with a special muscle in my skull. When I shut my eyes, the muscle pulls them downward into my head cavity. I also have a unique mouth. Instead of teeth, God formed the roof of my mouth with rows of ridges, which help smash and grind my meals.

God thought of everything when he created me—**Tomato Frog.**

More on the Web

Here I am, posing with a pal at the Fort Worth, Texas zoo.

http://whozoo.org/Intro2000/arnewiss/AW_tomatofrog.html

Tell a Friend

The tomato frog changes during bad weather. Sometimes our friends change when life gets difficult. Some people only want to be your friend when times are good. These people are known as "fair-weather friends." Aren't you glad God is not like that?

Read About It

"I give you a new command. Love one another. You must love one another, just as I have loved you."—John 13:34

If the temperature turns unseasonably warm or cold, I have a simple solution— I hibernate.

Pray About It

Lord, thank you for sticking with me during the good times and the bad times. Help me to be a faithful friend to others no matter what they are going through.

A Gentle Aussie Giant

I glide gracefully through the water off Australia, thanks to my skirt-like fins. They're thin and hang in billowing folds along my sides. When I squirt a jet of water out of special funnels, watch out! The water hits those fins and propels me forward. By pumping water in and out of my gas-filled cuttlebone, I am able to control how deep or shallow I glide through the water.

I'm the biggest type of cuttlefish, reaching a length of over three feet. Two gigantic eyes stare out at my world from my broad, flat head. Ten tentacles extend from my head also, waving like arms in an underwater ballet. Two are feeding tentacles, which can be reeled in when I'm done foraging. How's that for a portable fishing pole?

God taught me how to protect myself against predators. He gave me the ability to change the color and texture of my skin to imitate rock, sand, or plant. Or, I can sink to the bottom and rapidly pump water out of my funnels to bury myself in the sand.

If all else fails, I'll shoot a blob of an inky substance as a decoy, or create a cloud of ink in hopes of escaping behind it.

God thought of everything when he created me—**Giant Australian Cuttlefish.**

More on the Web

These low-light photos are amazing!

http://is.dal.ca/~ceph/TCP/Sapama.html

Tell a Friend

Actors memorize lines and try to imitate the character they are portraying—like the cuttlefish imitates rocks, sand, and plants. But God doesn't want you to pretend with him, since he already knows everything about you. You should always be honest with God.

Read About It

"God is spirit. His worshippers must worship him in spirit and in truth."—John 4:24

Pray About It

Lord, you know me better than anyone does. I'm glad I can relax and just be myself with you.

Underneath my fins and tentacles is a spongy, chalk-like shell called a cuttlebone. It gives shape to my body like a skeleton.

Too Hot to Handle!

S tand back, you ant! I have a boiling-hot surprise for you—a stinky toxic spray that I can aim perfectly, no matter where you try to bite me.

German scientists discovered that my body manufactures two special chemicals. Alone, the chemicals are not harmful— but combine them and *KABOOM!* An explosion takes place that results in the trigger-fast release of my chemical spray.

Each chemical is stored in a separate chamber along with a third chemical, called an *inhibitor*, which prevents them from exploding too soon. A tightly fitted ring of muscle separates the chambers. I relax the muscle when an enemy approaches, which allows the chemicals to flow together. Like a skilled chef, I add one final ingredient—a fourth chemical—which sends a message that it's time for an explosion.

Researchers from Cornell University used a special camera to record how fast I could respond to a predator. They poked and

prodded me with a small pair of forceps to imitate an ant attack. Each poke brought a perfectly aimed spray to the forceps.

No matter where the researchers poked me, I knew how to swivel my abdomen and discharge the spray to the exact spot. My amazing weapon never missed its mark.

God thought of everything when he created me—**Bombardier Beetle.**

More on the Web

See photos of me in action by Cornell University researchers:

http://news.bbc.co.uk/hi/english/sci/tech/newsid_422000/422599.stm

Tell a Friend

The bombardier beetle has a weapon that guarantees victory over ant attacks. The beetle's weapon is fast and always accurate. The Word of God is described as a spiritual weapon. It protects us from spiritual attacks that try to destroy our trust in the Lord.

Read About It

"The word of God is living and active. It is sharper than any sword that has two edges."—Hebrews 4:12

I carry enough chemicals at any given time to fire off 20 to 30 shots, one right after the other.

Pray About It

Thank you, God, for providing the Bible as a strong weapon for those of us who have placed our trust in you.

Life Inside the Slime

I hail from the coast of Ireland, where I live inside a thick, slimy tube buried on a beach. I am found in sheltered harbors or other areas that don't have a lot of foot traffic. You might also find me tucked under tiny rock ledges near starfish or anemones in a tide pool.

I grow to about eight inches long and one inch wide. If a predator bothers me, I can pull back inside my protective tube. I do this by shortening the length of my body to half its normal size, similar to the way a turtle behaves when it retreats into its shell. God taught me to filter water through my gills in order to catch anything worth eating. I'll dine on plankton or other small food that happens to float by me.

A giant nerve fiber stretches the entire length of my body. It is one of the largest nerve fibers in the animal kingdom. Because this nerve is so big, scientists are happy to study as many of us worms as possible. By inserting special probes into our bodies, they can test

how fast our nerves are able to conduct electricity.

God thought of everything when he created me—**Slime Worm.**

More on the Web

Here I am, soaking up some sun on a beach:

http://www.divebums.com/FishID/Pages/sabellid_worm.html

Tell a Friend

When trouble shows up, the slime worm does a disappearing act. What about you? How do you handle discouraging times? God has good advice for both good times and not-so-good times—keep trusting in him!

Read About It

"The Lord is good. When people are in trouble, they can go to him for safety. He takes good care of those who trust in him."—Nahum 1:7

Pray About It

Dear God, you are worthy of my trust. Thank you for hearing and answering my prayers.

In Psalms 22:6-8, King David cries out to God in his time of need. He says that his people are treating him poorly, "like a worm."

Stare Down with a Gecko

A couple of years ago, my mother laid two eggs on the African island of Mauritius. The eggs were connected, and she held them pressed tightly together with her hind legs until their shells hardened. Then she abandoned them. Two to three months later, my brother and I entered the world as hatchlings.

Life is one journey after another, but I am well-equipped. My toes are padded with bristly, microscopic hairs. At the end of each bristle, God installed between 100 and 1,000 tiny suction cups which allow me to walk up walls and cross ceilings upside-down.

I am one of the world's smallest reptiles. My scaly covering is designed in a pattern of striking colors like blue, red, orange, gold, and green. I look more like an ornate beaded purse than a reptile.

If you and I were to have a staring contest, I would win. My oversized eyes don't have lids, so I never blink! Fortunately, God gave me a long, sticky tongue that keeps my eyes moist and clean.

During the day, I forage for food while I hop along tree branches. At night, I find a smooth branch where I can sleep. I know a lot of predators would love a tender "geckowich" for dinner. But if an enemy grabs me, my tail breaks off and I scamper away. I don't worry, because another tail will grow back in a few days!

God thought of everything when he created me—**Ornate Day Gecko.**

More on the Web

See why reptile fans love me?

http://www.reptilecenter.com/geckoes/phelsuma_ornata_biology.htm

Tell a Friend

When someone hurts or annoys us, wouldn't it be nice to be able to leave the "broken" part behind, like the gecko? Life doesn't work that way, but the Bible does give us guidelines for handling sticky situations. Read about it below.

Read About It

"You have heard that it was said, 'Love your neighbor. Hate your enemy.' But here is what I tell you. Love your enemies. Pray for those who hurt you."—Matthew 5:43, 44

Day geckos like me benefit humans by helping to control the insect population.

Pray About It

Thank you for sending Jesus as an example of true love. Help me to love and forgive others just as Jesus does.

Neighborhood Snoop

What bird drops walnuts onto a busy highway so cars can run over the nuts and crack their shells? It's me—a bird that is considered crafty, intelligent, and an extreme pest.

Nothing escapes my notice. I perch at the top of trees to spy on other birds that are building nests. My brain records the location of each nest. I also watch birds carrying food back and forth to their babies. Many a nest has been robbed of its tasty young because of my sharp memory.

My feathers are a purplish-black color, but my bill, legs, and claws are pure black. I don't migrate during the winter, since the cold weather doesn't bother me. I prefer to nest in a clump of trees, but I have been known to nest on top of electrical power transformers, too. When I locate a good-looking tree with plenty of privacy, it becomes my roost. I share this special place with other members of my family. We eat an amazing variety of foods like cherries, acorns, walnuts,

birds, eggs, spiders, earthworms, fish, and small mammals.

I have a sharp eye for fishing. I can pick a fish out of the water—even from a fast-moving river or stream. I let nothing go to waste. If I spot a dead fish floating in the river, dinner is served!

God thought of everything when he created me—**Carrion Crow.**

More on the Web

Check out this glamour shot!

http://animalpicturesarchive.com/animal/ViewImg.cgi?img=a5/Carrion_crow1-by_MKramer.jpg

Tell a Friend

The carrion crow keeps his eye on everyone else's nest. People who spend all their time minding other people's business are sometimes called "snoops." In one of Paul's letters to the church at Thessalonica, he cautions church members to stay busy to avoid turning into snoops. His advice is good for us today, too.

Read About It

"Do everything you can to live a quiet life. Mind your own business. Work with your hands, just as we told you to. Then unbelievers will have respect for your everyday life."—1 Thessalonians 4:11, 12

The Bible mentions birds' nests in the New Testament when it describes Jesus as having no place to rest. Read Matthew 8:20.

Pray About It

Lord, help me to learn the difference between snoopiness, and being genuinely concerned about others. Show me ways I can help those who need help.

My Sticky Zigzag Surprise

Stand back, I'm a spitter! I belong to a family of six-eyed spiders. If you live in Singapore, I might have my eyes on you!

No need to worry. I'm harmless to humans, although if you stumble upon me in the night, it might be a creepy meeting. I'm a hairless spider that packs some very heavy equipment. I have a venom gland in front and a sticky silk-shooter in back.

While other insects sleep, I roam through the night hunting for a victim. In spite of all those eyes, my vision is poor, so God provided long sensory hairs on my feet. I crawl with my front legs raised, feeling my way around in the dark. Scientists believe that I am able to detect a victim nearby, as well as judge how far away it is, thanks to those hairs. I then react quickly—no time to waste!

I can attack a moth before it even knows I'm around by squeezing

the back of my body together and spitting out two poisonous silk threads. I spit them in a split-second burst, zigzagging the strands over my victim like a fancy net. The sticky silk not only glues my prey in place, it paralyzes it so I can move in for a fatal bite. Once my victim dies, I then peel away the silk strands. Let the picnic begin!

God thought of everything when he created me—**Spitting Spider.**

More on the Web

Check out this photo of one night's catch:

http://www.the-piedpiper.co.uk/th11f(9).htm

Tell a Friend

The spitting spider creeps around at night seeking out something to devour. That's how Satan tries to catch us off guard. He wraps sin up in a pretty disguise and tries to tell us it's OK just this once. But God invites us to run to him when we are tempted. In him, we can find safety and rest.

Read About It

"So obey God. Stand up to the devil. He will run away from you. Come near to God, and he will come near to you."—James 4:7

After laying eggs, my mother carried them around in her fangs for two weeks. Joined together by several silky strands, her precious cargo rode in what looked like a lacy little purse. I hatched two weeks later.

Pray About It

It is good to know that you are just a prayer away, Lord! When I am tempted, help me to turn away and run straight to you for help.

Flightless Parrot
of the Night

At eight pounds, I hold the title for world's heaviest parrot. I am also one of the strangest and rarest birds in the world. You won't see me soaring through the air, since I am a flightless parrot. I am also *nocturnal*, which means I am active during the night and sleep all through the day.

My scientific name is a mouthful: *strigops habroptilus.* Aren't you glad your name is simple? My name means "owl-like," which is exactly what I am. My feathers are soft like an owl's, and I have a puffy circle of bristly feathers around my face.

When the first Europeans arrived in New Zealand around two hundred years ago, they brought along new animals like ferrets, weasels, and feral cats. These creatures hit the island running, and soon developed an appetite for my family members. Since we are

considered endangered animals, my little family now lives in a special habitat where we are kept safe and sound.

I have small, stumpy wings that are useless for flying. But when I am jumping down a steep bank, they sure come in handy for steering! Natives say I smell sweet and spicy, too.

God thought of everything when he created me—**Kakapo.**

More on the Web

Aren't these two kakapo chicks adorable?

http://www.doc.govt.nz/Whats-New/E-Cards/img/card_5.jpg

Tell a Friend

The kakapo is not a typical bird. It is a unique species—one of a kind. People are also unique. But we do have one very special thing in common: the need for a Savior. God knew our need and loved us enough to send Jesus for that very purpose! Read about it in the verse below.

Read About It

"God loved the world so much that he gave his one and only Son. Anyone who believes in him will not die but will have eternal life."

—John 3:16

The Bible mentions feathers and wings in Psalm 91:4. Read what God says about his loving protection over us.

Pray About It

Lord, thank you for creating me as a unique individual. And thank you for sending Jesus to be my Savior.

Big Shot of the Forest

S cientist don't know whether to call me a plant, animal, or fungus. I live in rotting stumps and downed logs deep in the forest. I'm a member of a family known as *slime molds*. My family lives in every continent of the world, as part of God's design.

During a certain stage of growth, I send up tiny growths that resemble miniature mushrooms. In the autumn, you will find me growing in neat rows along a downed tree or in the cracks of a stump. You might also find me growing under leaf litter or on large twigs scattered across the forest floor.

During my *fruiting* stage, I am filled with a creamy, slimy substance that resembles a thick milkshake. Hungry insect larvae love to scoop out my innards and feast on my scrumptious slime mold.

I change in size, shape, and color as I grow. My "costumes" range in color from gold to white to orange to brown. Photographers and painters have captured me on film and canvas. I'm sort of a

forest celebrity, since I've been the star of many books and educational videos.

If I can escape those hungry insect larvae, I will live long enough to feed on decaying materials in the forest. What do you suppose would happen to all those rotting logs and stumps if it wasn't for tiny workers like me?

God thought of everything when he created me—**Ice Cream Cone Myxo.**

More on the Web
Join a Smithsonian team on a slime mold hunt.

http://www.smithsonianmag.si.edu/smithsonian/issues01/mar01/phenom_mar01.html

Tell a Friend
Each stage of a slime mold's growth brings about change. As we grow, we will also change in size and appearance. But the most important growth happens in our spirit, where only God can see. Are you learning to depend more on him each day?

Read About It
"Grow in the grace of our Lord and Savior Jesus Christ. Get to know him better."—2 Peter 3:18

Scientists are studying one of my slimy cousins to see how its cells grow, in hopes of understanding how diseases like cancer spread.

Pray About It
Give me a hunger for your Word, Lord, so I can get to know you better.

Cool books for preteens!

SURVIVING
MIDDLE SCHOOL
written by
Sandy Silverthorne
0-7847-1433-9

BELIEVE IT!
written by
Steven James
0-7847-1393-6

GOD THOUGHT OF
EVERYTHING
AND WACKY
itten by
ie Bruno
7-1447-9

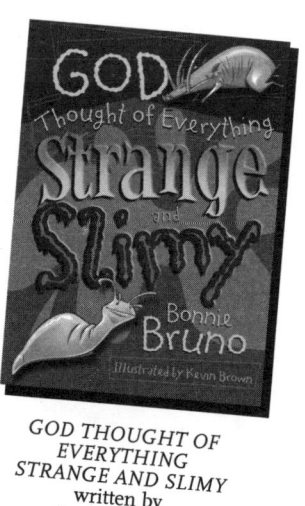

GOD THOUGHT OF
EVERYTHING
STRANGE AND SLIMY
written by
Bonnie Bruno
0-7847-1448-7